Whispers
OF THE
HEART

TRISHA CAMPBELL

outskirts
press

Table of Contents

Introduction

SOMETIMES IN OUR lives, unforeseen circumstances happen that we may not understand. Whether it is an unexpected illness, trauma from an accident, the death of a loved one, or a child that is diagnosed with special needs, it all can come as quite a shock.

It is in those unprecedented times of heartbreak, when your words don't come out easily and every ache of your heart can leave you feeling so alone and broken, that you realize what you are really made of and Who it is that made you.

At times, you may find yourself reaching a point where your heart cries out so desperately that it surfaces in painful whispers of tears puddling on the floor from your weathered and tattered soul. These painful whispers of the heart are so deep that others would not or just could not understand even if they tried. Your despondent spirit then continuously cries out to God for help to get through the unexpected.

If you are wondering how I know this, well, it's because my family and I have experienced a lot of these exact circumstances that at times have left us questioning if we could walk another step in this journey that we call life. Just when it seemed like things were settling down a bit, another test of faith would find us. It was in these times of unexpected circumstances that I had to dig deep for any faith and hope that I could find for my unsettled heart.

At times, I have found myself searching way down to the depths of my very own soul to move forward and understand and deal with my heartbreak and tears; all the while realizing that even though circumstances at times appeared bleak, somehow with God's help, I found the strength needed to face another day.

Blessings can sometimes come through teardrops. Strength and life lessons sometimes come through pain. Our attitude and our reactions to situations during these times can either make or break us.

Faith, hope, and a strong-willed determination have all collectively played a huge part in the lives of both me and my husband in our marriage as well as in our lives through cancer, various unexpected illnesses, tragedy, death, and the challenges and blessings of our very own son with special needs.

To help set a foundation and understand the journey of hope and faith throughout this book, it is in my heart to share with you not only our journey, but to also share how God has been a constant even when we felt alone and questioned our faith in times of great despair.

During moments of the unexpected, it's difficult to see that there is an anchor of hope that can be thrown out to keep you from drowning. As you seem to suffocate from the feelings of intense heartache, it may be that your circumstances are too painful for others to understand or too painfully intense for you to share with them in fear of being judged or misunderstood.

I, too, have felt this way so many times in my personal journey. To be openly honest and reach out for help sometimes sounds easier than it truly is. However, as hard as it is at times, I have learned in my own personal journey that in sharing both the struggles faced in this life as well as the victories experienced, others can gain courage and strength to reach out to share their own victories even in the middle of their pain.

Words have power. Our words may be the very encouragement that someone else needs to hear that motivates them to keep going. Our hope may be what pulls someone out of a pit of despair. If we can help someone else with our very own stories, why would we not reach out to offer hope to them and help rescue them with our very own lifeline of faith?

Thank you for the opportunity to share with you my "Whispers of the Heart". I hope that this book both encourages and challenges you to reach deep within, find your hope and inner faith, and reach out to share your very own personal story that may help to release someone else's "heart whispers."

Trisha Campbell

1

"God," "Where are You?"

IF YOU HAVE ever experienced difficulty in any form, then you've realized that life's circumstances can throw out some really tough times. Circumstances that can certainly test our faith and make us question God about his plan and will for our life. To have a hopeful heart is a sign that you are keeping your head above water. Or is it?

Do you hold it all together in front of everyone else knowing that deep down inside at any second you could just explode or just fall into a million pieces? Have you ever felt hopeless knowing no matter what you do, you can't fix it or make it all disappear?

If you've ever felt like this, then you will understand how it feels to want to pray, but no matter how hard you try to talk to God, it seems that the words always come out in tiny whispers surrounded by tears puddling in your floor as your broken heart tries to understand God's plan for your life.

This, my friends, will give you a glimpse of what it's like to feel hopeless. Others may think you have it all together, but deep down you and God know differently. What's even worse is feeling an overwhelming weakness in the middle of your hopelessness as Satan targets you at your weakest point and vulnerability and you start to believe his lies. You whisper to yourself that you are helpless in your situation. You find yourself focusing on the problems and not on the Problem Solver.

Then, as you begin to doubt that the God who is supposed to love you is even listening to your heartbreak, you begin to question in your life's circumstances why God's plan would include sickness, pain, and hurt. Somehow, you try to remind yourself that there must be more to this life and your story than this and that God will never leave you, but your weary spirit is just tired.

When the questions surface and you begin to wonder why the God that you love and serve would allow circumstances that are painful and tragic to happen in your life, it's so easy to find blame. Deep down, as a child of God, you know you must take Him at His Word but sometimes you find yourself with lip service just going through the motions. As you try to put on a brave face in the presence of others and look deep inside to try to remind yourself that there must be a reason for these circumstances, you are truly hoping you can get through the day without falling apart. While you are soul searching, you begin thinking, "There has to be a plan and a purpose in all of this, even in all the pain and struggle, somehow, somewhere."

This is how I've felt many times throughout my life. Holding it all together on the outside, falling apart on the inside, yet somehow finding a deep-rooted hope and faith that God placed in my soul by reaching some very low times and crying out to God in my desperation. In life, we have the option to hope or despair. We can choose to find joy or live defeated. Understanding the difference between joy and happiness is hard at times but it is vital to getting out of a depression pit. Joy is a deeply rooted emotion that comes from knowing that even in life's despondency, there is a hope to make it through. Happiness, however, is based on circumstances alone.

In the heat of a hard moment, it's hard to see past our current circumstances and areas of struggle. Our focus gets shifted and we wonder if we will ever see the light at the end of our very long and dark tunnel.

When my heart has crumbled to the very lowest point where only whispers can reach God and the words just can't come out, my heart reminds me of Scripture and how God's Word can combat any lie that

Satan tries to throw my way.

One day as I was feeling very low and vulnerable, God reminded me that the Holy Spirit Himself intercedes for us with "groanings" which cannot be uttered.

It's then that I thought to myself, "So...God, let me get this straight, YOU are telling me that YOU understand my pain? YOU understand my 'heart whispers?' YOU understand my desperation and heart cries? YOU are prompting the Holy Spirit Himself to intercede for me right now by crying out for me since I can't find the words myself at this very moment? You really love me this much?

*Then, Lord, if this is true, why can't **YOU** just fix it all?*

'GOD?'
"Where are you?"

As my whispers are then yelling out to God in my desperation from my troubled heart, I grab my Bible and in desperation find the Scripture in Romans 8:26 which says, *"Likewise the Spirit helps us in our infirmities and weaknesses, for we do not know what we should pray for as we ought, but the Spirit Himself is making intercession for us with groanings that cannot be uttered."* Hmmm. Groanings…. Sounds like God Himself even understands the emotion of despair and heartbreak, doesn't it? But if so and this is true, why do I feel so all alone?

As my mind wrestles within me, and even as His promises are right there in front of me and I know that His promises are true, so many times I have found myself questioning where God is in all of it. I have even driven down the road in my car alone yelling in frustration and desperation at God and asking, "God, where are You? What are You doing? Why is all of this happening? "

The Bible teaches us that God is ever-present, meaning He is always near us. We are also told in Scripture that God never leaves us or forsakes us. So, as I wrestle within myself, I remind myself of these promises and start to ponder the story, "The Footprints." I feel like a woman on the beach, walking alone, so weak, and alone in fact, that I cannot stand. A lot of times I find myself falling to the ground -discouraged, despondent, and desperate.

As I argue with God, I am telling Him, "God, You promised! You promised to take care of me and my family and right now I'm feeling so alone and my trust in you and your promises are dwindling. I am weak. I am tired. I am confused. I feel alone. I need strength."

"GOD?"
"Are You Here?"

In these darkest days of my life, I am reminded that Yes, God Himself, is HERE! He is carrying me even when I don't feel Him near or see situations being resolved at that moment, He is SUPERNATURALLY working out situations that my human mind can't even imagine. Jesus Himself has had to be my strength and pick me back up when at times I have wanted to give up. He has had to pick up my pieces of my broken heart and put them back together on more than one occasion.

"So, God, why? What are you doing? How am I supposed to be okay in all of this?" Have you ever been there? Be honest. I know that I have, and I have truly questioned and cried and begged and pleaded and tried to figure out what God was even thinking and how it could ever be beneficial.

Now, before you go fabricating in your head how I shouldn't be questioning God or His plan for my life, I want to remind you of a few things that may enlighten you to understand how a relationship with God works.

If you are a Christian or have been a Christian for any length of time at all, then you realize that God is truly your Heavenly Father and that you are His daughter or son and because of this you have a Father and son or daughter relationship. I'm sure that growing up in your own house with your own family you had questions about things in life just as I did. Were you afraid to ask those that were closest to you, I mean the ones who really cared about you, the whys? You found yourself needing comfort, reassurance, and guidance and so you reached out, right? Well, why then, can we not reach out to our Heavenly Father in ALL circumstances, emotions, feelings, and cares? The Bible says in 1 Peter 5:7 that we can *"Cast all our anxieties on Him, because He cares for us."*

So why then, is this so hard? Why does my faith feel so weak when I know in my heart God is near as I question this in my own spirit? Friends, I am human. I am dust. I, just like you, wrestle with emotions and struggles and that's okay. God truly understands our innermost being. I've found when I feel this "human" ness in myself that it makes me thankful to know that my own sufficiency is not enough. If I were a perfect individual, then why would I have a need for God?

It's then that I realize that I need Him. Jesus. His Presence. His comfort. His guidance. His love. It's then that I understand that God is there to hold me as I cry "Abba, Father." It's then that I surrender in tears as my heart breaks within me knowing He will put my life back together, in His time and in His way.

I may not see it yet, but the answers are coming. Peace is coming. Strength is coming. Hope is just up ahead. So, how do I get past this Hope"less"ness? I must pursue God. I must find a quiet place to focus on Him and my relationship with the God that loves me. What better place to find peace and solitude than in those quiet moments with the Lord and His Word? It was on a day such as this that I needed to be reminded and as I dug deep into Scripture, Jesus gave me Words from His Holy Book. I began to study and read the story in Matthew 26 like I never had before.

2

How To Turn Hope"less"ness into Hope"full"ness

THIS STORY FOUND in Matthew 26:36-42 spoke to me on such a desperate day in my life. I found hope, peace, and comfort, even in the hard and desperate situations that I was facing. As I looked deep into the story, I was reminded of the context in Scripture, beginning with the events that are leading up to the death of Jesus. Jesus was scolded by His disciples when He was taking some time to visit with Simon the leper and a woman came up to Him with an alabaster box of very expensive perfume. She poured out the perfume, washed Jesus' feet with it, and even wiped his feet with her hair.

One of Jesus' disciples was angry at this point and complaining as he was telling Jesus that this lady had wasted perfume that could have been sold with the profit being distributed to the poor. He was upset to witness such a senseless act, yet he himself would later betray Jesus as a traitor.

Mary, however, knew that Jesus had helped her, saved, her, and redeemed her. Jesus didn't judge her. He knew in His Spirit that she had the assurance that she had been helped, healed, and forgiven, and in her heart cries she knew that Jesus was the only One who could have helped her in her own heart cries to Jesus, Himself.

Jesus then told His disciples to *"Leave her alone,"* and explained to them what they could not see with their physical eyes. Supernaturally, He knew that she truly had come to a point in her life where she knew that she was healed from sinfulness and had received such hope that she was ready to pour out all she had before Jesus in worship and adoration. She had the faith to believe and remembered the day that Jesus had healed and forgiven her.

Jesus had also used her example as a testament of His body and burial that was coming. Jesus Himself knew what was coming. He knew Mary had just poured out the desperate whispers of her heart. She was redeemed, she was forgiven. Someone who had no idea about a life filled with righteousness knew in her spirit and in her desperation that when she cried out to the Savior, He answered and delivered.

As the complaining stopped, the disciples continued to walk with Jesus to begin on their journey to The Lord's Supper. Judas, the same man that complained about Mary and was supposed to be loyal to Jesus was about to betray Him for thirty pieces of silver. Someone who knew the way of righteousness yet chose the ways of sin. Someone who was supposed to be faithful to God's calling yet turned on Jesus when Jesus needed Him the most.

Once they arrived at the supper, Jesus sat down with His twelve friends. Knowing a betrayal from Judas was coming, He mentions that one of them would betray Him. In utter shock, they all questioned who it was that would be the backstabber. Who it was that was two-faced and would do such a horrific thing? Judas knew in his heart what he was about to do. But in a hypocritical tone, he said, *"Rabbi, is it I?"*

Jesus validated it even though Judas knew he was the one and Judas then betrayed Jesus with a kiss on his cheek in exchange for thirty pieces of silver. No wonder he was complaining about Mary and her "waste" as he watched in disbelief how the expensive perfume was poured out in honor of Jesus. Money became more important to him at that very moment than friendship. Sometimes people in our lives that we think are our friends and have our very best interest at heart end up being the ones who betray us. That's why at times we learn to guard our hearts and are afraid to reach out to others in fear of betrayal. I, myself, have learned this more than once in my life. It's tough, but you learn to heal and trust again.

In the context of the story though, I am also reminded of the other disciples. A lot of times we focus on Judas in the story because he was a traitor. I try to remember the loyalty of the other disciples as they tried to honor Jesus. Even though they made their share of mistakes, they all knew that they loved Jesus and continued to try to be faithful to the call that Jesus had on their lives even though they, at times, struggled and strayed along the way.

While I've learned that it's very important to "guard your heart" because a lot of people in today's time will prey on vulnerability, there are still the "few true" that you will find to be loyal. There are still a few that will come alongside of you in your struggles and unexpected circumstances and offer a shoulder and lend a helping hand. It always seems that God in His infinite love and wisdom will always place the right person in your path at just the right time and just at that moment when you need them the most.

There will also, however, be times when no one can physically understand your pain and anguish no matter how hard they try. There will still be times of loneliness and fear and frustration. It is then that defeat as well as desperation wants to creep into your heart through Satan's lies and tell you it's "hopeless". He wants you to feel so "helpless" that you feel no one could ever understand nevertheless help you at that very moment.

"But GOD,"
"He is there!"

Yes, He is there. He is waiting. He is listening. As your heart cries turn to whispers, He is listening and ready to help mend your broken heart and put the pieces back together. You may not physically see it; however, He is willing and ready to help. He feels and hears your heart cries. He promised to never leave or forsake you. In your darkest moments, He is holding you up and sends an army of angels to help you fight the difficulties with His strength. The most desperate and vulnerable heart will be encouraged to know that hope"less"ness can be anchored in hope"full"ness. The lifeline of God can restore any damaged and broken spirit and break the strongholds of Satan.

"Oh God!"
"You are here!"

We are promised that God will give us strength. In Isaiah 41:10, He tells us that we don't have to be afraid. He is our God and our Refuge, and He will uphold us with His hands as we are falling into that pit of desperation and depression.

As the story in Matthew continues, the disciples sit down with Jesus at the Last Supper. Although they didn't fully understand what was coming for Jesus, He was trying to prepare them for his death and burial. The Last Supper was the very first communion. Many churches of many different affiliations still celebrate the sacrament of the communion.

If you've never thought about "Communion" in this light, think about this for a minute. Jesus' very "Last" was our very "First". I don't know about you, but that resonates my spirit with Hope. Because of Jesus death, we in turn, have a "very first" for an eternal life in Heaven with Him.

The heartfelt symbolism at the Communion table, I'm sure, was watched in awe and surprise when the laughter and celebrating at the supper took a serious tone. As Jesus took the bread and brake it, He implied the symbolism of "His very body being broken on the cross". Jesus signified the importance of "His blood being shed for sin" through the symbolism of the juice. The disciples would not fully understand this symbolism until a bit later when it would become a reality as they would watch Jesus suffer on the cross.

Even in the very "sadness" of His "last", Jesus made a way for our very "first". It's because of His shed blood on Calvary and His body being broken for our sins that we have an atonement made for us. No matter how sinful we have been, no matter how angry we have been, no matter how argumentative and frustrated we have been, He still loved us enough to take His "last" to make our "first". Even down to His very last breath.

I'm so very thankful, though, that the story doesn't end there. We serve a Risen Savior! A Savior Who not only experienced "death" in a most horrific and cruel way, but One Who also made a way for us to experience eternal life through the Power of His Resurrection. The Hope that we have in Jesus' return to take us home to Heaven is one that should pull anyone out of a pit of despair. I'm so thankful this isn't the end. We have hope. This physical place we call home is only temporary; Heaven is eternal.

Salvation is free. It is an eternal gift that God provided to us as sinners. We must know that we are not sufficient within ourselves. We fall so short of God's grace and mercy daily.

Christ can indeed, turn our Hope "less" ness into Hope "full" ness. As I look at myself in a mirror and think of how insufficient I am at times, it's in those moments that my *insufficiency* gives me hope. Sounds a bit like an oxymoron, doesn't it? It's just that in that very weak moment, I realize that I am not qualified to understand or know the reasons of situations beyond my control. I'm reminded of **JESUS** and **HIS POWER**. He chose to take His very last breath on the Cross because He loved me and wanted me to be sufficient in Him. He knew I would need a Redeemer and a Savior. He knew that I would need Someone who had been broken both in Body and in Spirit to understand my pain.

I knew in my heart cries as I read this Scripture text that if Jesus, Himself, could feel MY emotions, then He also surely could help me in death to this despair within myself and raise me again to life. I knew He could give me joy even in life's most painful and disheartening circumstances if I would only surrender my all. To surrender all the feelings, emotions, pain, and heartbreak that has built up in your soul isn't easy. Again, at times, these feelings can only be spoken in a language of tears puddling around you as your heart cries out in whispers, that at times, only God Himself can hear.

3

Jesus' Heart Whispers in the Garden of Gethsemane

AS I CONTINUED my reading in Matthew's Gospel, I realized just how much Jesus was human/ yet God and how He felt every emotion ever known to humankind. I was amazed to know that Jesus Himself understood my heart whispers even down to the very depths of my soul. As many times as I've heard this story about Jesus in the Garden or even all the many times that this passage has been read in the Bible as I've listened in church, it never really hit me like it did until this very day when I read this passage again in my Bible on a day that I needed assurance and comfort. I never really thought about Jesus and how He felt until the Holy Spirit guided me to understand the struggle of Jesus Himself in the Garden.

I was "wowed" as I read that in the desperation in the Garden, Jesus, Himself, had his own heart cries to His very own Father. Jesus in His love had come to redeem us, knowing his fate, yet chose to continue with the plan. The disciples and Jesus had finished their meal and as the story tells us, they continued walking on course toward the "The Garden of Gethsemane". Jesus knew that he was about to die. He knew what He was about to experience and He, being human, yet God, felt the anxiety and heartbreak, as well as the anguish.

Really? You may ask? Jesus felt human emotions? Yes, absolutely, He sure did even down to the tears and heartbreak of life that seemed so very heavy to Him at this point in the Scripture. It is very evident in both His speech and in His body language when He asked his disciples to sit and wait on him. He told them that His soul was exceedingly sorrowful even unto death. Then, He walks into the Garden **ALONE.**

The Bible says, "*He fell on his face*" .... I view that as **desperation, heartbreak, turmoil,** and **sadness**. He cries out to His Father and says, *"Oh My Father if it is possible, let this cup pass from me; nevertheless, not as I will, but as You will."*

He then continued as he prays a second and third time, "If this cup cannot pass away from Me unless I drink it, Thy will be done." Wow. Sounds like Jesus Himself had His own "whispers of the heart" doesn't it? Sounds like he was questioning the "plan". Sounds like to me he was agonizing with His very own Father, God Himself, as He tells God, in His own desperation that He knew the plan but wasn't sure He could withstand the heartbreak. His heart cried out to God as his sweat became as great drops of blood falling to the ground (found in Luke 22:44).

Was this literal or just figurative? Can tears really become blood? If you take the time to research this, you may be amazed to know that it is truly physically possible! The process of sweating blood is called "Hematohidrosis" and to cry tears of blood is called "Hemolacria". Both have been physically known to happen with individuals under extreme levels of stress when facing death!

Wow! So, yes, even Christ Himself faced heartbreak even down to the physical, emotional, and spiritual emotions that turned to drops of blood falling to the ground from the depths of His very own soul.

"Thy will be done". Hard words to pray. Hard words to understand; however, Jesus knew He needed to be willing and obedient to fulfill God's plan for us. He looked down in time and loved us so much that He would face his horrific death on the cross to give us Salvation. He knew as hard as this was to face, He would be raised to life again. He knew that the suffering and despondency of this life was only

temporary and that He would make a way for us to know Him and live with Him in eternity forever in His love and in His presence!

"WOW GOD!!!!!"
"YOU DO UNDERSTAND!!!!!"

As I continued to read, my heart cries turned to tears of thankfulness. I was in such adoration that Jesus Himself understood me with all my emotions and all my baggage. He understood and because of this assurance I found peace and comfort. Heart cries, "Whispers of the Heart" are found when we seem to be at our lowest points and can't seem to understand the purpose behind what is happening. Oh, the life lessons that can be learned through tears and the hope and stamina that can be proven through pain, even on the hardest days!

Although we, as humans, are not sufficient in ourselves, we can depend on the sufficiency of Christ. We may not have it all together and may be falling apart, but He holds us up and cradles us in His arms. We are not able to see the future, but He sees it and He knows what we need to help us to walk another step even to the point of carrying us when we can't make it on our own. We may feel insignificant, but His promise in 2 Corinthians 12:9 tells us that "His grace is sufficient for us; His strength is made perfect in our weaknesses."

Each day is a gift that we are given to use our stories to reach out and help others and show them the light at the end of their deepest darkest tunnel. So, even while it hurts and the weight of life is heavy, with tests that are difficult to pass, there is a reason for the struggle. Hope"less"ness, and heartbreak will come with the desperation and the struggle to stay afloat. Times will be difficult, challenges will be hard, you may feel like quitting, but to stay in that state of mind should never be an option.

How can we ever muster up the courage to face our problems and fight back to defeat Hope"less"ness head-on? How do we defeat the lies of Satan and move forward to a new day? **GO BACK.** Have your mind walk backwards and step into the journey of the past.

REMEMBER. Look at your life circumstances. Remember the times you thought you would never make it through a particular moment or circumstance, and you did? *Remember God's promises and yell them out over the lies of Satan!* God will never leave us. He will always be nearby. Not only a prayer away, but also a breath, a heart cry, a tear, a heart whisper…. He hears and sees them all.

One of Satan's greatest weapons against us is the battlefield of our minds. Ever heard of creating a new mind set? DO IT!!!! God never promised this life would be easy, but He did promise to be with us every single step of the way, even in those times of heart cries and defeat within ourselves.

So…… **STOP living defeated**! Focus on the positive and stop living that negative life. **Use your weapons! Put on your Armor!** The Bible tells us in Ephesians 6:10-18 how to suit up for Spiritual Warfare. We've got to be prepared. The attacks are going to come in this life. The enemy is always searching to destroy us.

Allow yourself some grace and time to heal and then pray for strength to help others and reach those who are hurting. Share God's "Hope"full"ness with others and let them know they are not alone. There is hope and faith to share in each of our stories to overcome the lies of Satan.

Your words may be the very lifeline someone needs to keep going. You may give them hope by sharing your story. You may save them from an overdose, a suicide, or a life filled with despair, bitterness, or hate. Your story can turn their" I can't's" into "I can's." Your story can turn their hope"less"ness into hope"full"ness. I felt the need to share our story as these emotions flooded my soul. My hope as you continue to read is to be encouraged and then look at your own life and share! *God can take our stories and use them for His glory.*

4

"Hallelujah, Even Here"

WHEN I STARTED writing this book over five years ago now, I wasn't sure how I would tell our family's story. I wanted to include all that has occurred with not only our little family of three but with the struggles of our parents and other family members through sickness, tragedy, and even at times, death for ultimate healing. God has been faithful even at times when I've been falling apart and haven't felt like I could even whisper a prayer.

It was then I realized that although writing was something that I have always enjoyed, writing this book has also proved as a therapy and a healing for me. As I started to write out how I was feeling and went through each circumstance that has happened, I would fill up with so much emotion that I would have to go away and cry a bit, get myself together, and come back to pen more words. I realized during those moments that I had not completely healed in a lot of areas myself and that I still needed to surrender my heart cries and emotions to God even more than I ever realized.

Originally, I had the order of the chapters of this book in a different sequence and honestly since I started penning the words, a lot of chapters have been edited or added to over the years in addition. With some recent circumstances and things that have happened, I recently had to add more to our story than I knew would ever be coming.

In the years that I have been writing this book with pauses and edits along the way, it's now the year 2021 and it's been about ten months ago now since I heard this song for the first time - "Hallelujah, Even Here." The singer and songwriter's name is Lydia Lard. As I listened to her testimonial from "The Girl Talk Podcast" of 106.9, the Light, I was amazed at how the words of this very song came to her as she was facing a difficult challenge in her own life. She was given a medical diagnosis and was told that she may lose her voice box. As I listened to her story of how she was raised in a Christian home, had trusted Christ at an early age, and had tried to live her life for the Lord I thought about my own journey and some similarities that we had. As I listened to her, I realized that she had questions and concerns and struggled just like me as the questions flooded her soul, and she had her own heart cries to God needing answers and reassurance.

I'm sure that she was feeling, hope"less" and help"less" as the lies of Satan played over in her mind, yet, she knew that God had a plan. She chose to take her situation, lay it out before God with all her questions, cry out to him in her heart cries of desperation and whispers of her heart as she penned the words to this song. She now sings in victory as her situation was handled by her almighty Creator with her voice that God healed in His way and in His timing.

The first time I heard the song, "Hallelujah Even Here", I was in my car. God and I have a car relationship some days. You know with music and podcasts and hearing the Word. As a special needs mom, wife, and teacher, I'm very busy sometimes just running on fumes. I have a home to maintain, school to handle, therapies for my son, a teaching position, as well as being a plugged-in wife to my wonderful husband of twenty-five years and my fourteen-year-old special needs son who desperately needs his mama. So, yes, a lot of times, even though I still make time to read God's Word and pray, some days God and I end up having some bonding time in my car rides as well as we travel along not only our physical journey in this life but in our spiritual connection as well.

So... it was on a day in my car that I heard this song as I was in desperation after a diagnosis: Hodgkin's Lymphoma. Ever heard of it? Well, it's a type of blood cancer. My husband had been diagnosed-STAGE IV with tumors that ranged from his lymph nodes in his neck, to his abdominal area, back, and bones. He was going to be facing port surgery, chemotherapy, and radiation.

Hearing the word, CANCER, as I sat in that office with my husband, I tried to hold it all together. It wasn't the first time that cancer had hit our family. My mom is a thirty-year cancer survivor. We had a previous scare a few years earlier in 2018 as my husband had some medical testing that resulted in elevated blood platelets where they ruled out cancer and leukemia and ultimately diagnosed Rick with Essential Thrombocytosis, which is a blood platelet disorder. Yet, here we sat three years later, hearing a diagnosis of CANCER-STAGE IV-HODGKINS LYMPHOMA.

As I sat there with Rick, I cried out in my spirit, "God? Did they miss something? Is this your plan? God, no, please no. What are you doing? I just don't understand. In my desperation and with my broken heart I am screaming from the inside,

"GOD?"
"Where are you?"

In my spirit, I'm telling God, "God, haven't we had enough? We have been through so much already in various areas with our own child's diagnosis of special needs, our parents and siblings that have struggled with Guillain' barre syndrome, Osteogenesis Imperfecta, Colon cancer, strokes, Huntington's disease, Heart attacks, Tragic accidents, and now Hodgkin's Lymphoma? Why God? I just don't get it. We have served You. We have tried to honor You. However, at this very moment, I feel like You are so far away."

As I sat in amazement at my husband in his faith, he tells the doctor, "I'm not sure where your faith is doc, but God's got it. I am going to be okay." In his optimistic and joking way, he says, "I'm not finished aggravating my wife yet, nor am I finished raising my special needs son and I will beat this."

Trying not to lose it sitting right in that doctor's office as my tears are welling up, I look away. The doctor is giving us the hopeful news that even in stage IV, with this particular type of cancer, it is usually very treatable and often times curable.

Again, Rick's faith amazes me. He says: "I will beat this. "God's got it". Even if I don't make it, God's got it. I know where I am going, but I know he's not finished with our story yet and I'm going to be just fine."

Boom……. As my heart is silently asking God where He is and what in the world He is doing at this point in our journey, I'm sitting in amazement listening to my husband and his faith and I realize that my heart cries once again are struggling in the desperation of my own soul that needs healing.

"GOD?"
"What is your purpose in all of this?"
"I am scared!"

As my thoughts race, I'm saying in my spirit, "God, I know you are faithful. I've watched your hands work through so many circumstances. I've seen miracles happen. I've witnessed your faithfulness, but, God, Why? I thought your answer was clear three years ago when they ruled out Leukemia. God, I just don't understand this. I need him! Brian needs him! I just can't do this, God. I just can't."

As the doctor visit ends, we both get into my husband's truck to leave as he drives me back to get my car. I parked in a different location meeting him at the doctor's office in between our schedules. I was fighting back the tears and trying not to lose it. Rick keeps reassuring me on the ride that God has us. He told me that he knew that God had not brought us this far in our journey to stop working now. He told me to trust God. He told me that God is good, even in this. He told me that he knew I still had my faith and that I could find it if I would only trust in God's plan. My heart, however, at that moment was shattering into a million pieces as I'm sitting and listening to this man who is the one who should be falling apart yet talks with such confidence and faith.

As he is talking and trying to encourage my heartbreak, I thought, I should be the strong one reassuring him, but my words were just stuck as I'm sitting beside him in shock and disbelief. Numb, if you understand that emotion. Holding his hand and caressing it I'm thinking he's the one with this diagnosis and yet as I'm the one struggling, I look at Rick and I see strength. I see courage. I see love. I see God. I thought, wow, my faith must just be horribly weak. What's wrong with me?

As he was talking, his strength reminded me of my dad who was my Pastor for many years. I grew up as a PK (Preacher's Kid). It was under my dad's leadership that I felt God tug on my heart at just seven years old. I became a Christian. I knew God. I loved God. I had and still have a very real relationship with God. But right then, at that very moment, I was deeply questioning my faith and I did not understand God's plan for our lives at all.

This doctor's appointment was at 12:30. As a teacher/ABA therapist in our local school district, I had taken the day off to be with my husband but also had a potential new job opportunity and had to make a final job interview at another school, Westminster Catawba Christian School, this very same afternoon at 1:30.

How in the world can I go to this interview, I thought? I am a wreck. My husband and I just got the worst news ever. I feel like the worst Christian ever. As I am questioning everything in my life at this point, my husband dropped me off at my car to go pick up my son from the school he attended at the time. As I kissed him and turned to leave, he reassured me that I needed to go on to this interview, telling me again, "Trish, God's got this. He has a plan. Trust Him." As I watched him drive away, my mind was racing. I knew I had to get to my interview, so I got in my car, numb with this news, and drove into the school parking lot.

This was going to be my final interview for a potential position, and I did not know if I would be offered a position at all, but I knew I had to try. So, here I was in my car now sitting in the parking lot of the school. I was trying to put on a brave face while holding back my tears, so my make-up didn't run down my cheeks and smear black eyeliner and mascara down my face before the interview. Coaching myself, I said, "Breathe. Just Breathe."

As I walked in, the Principal, Mrs. Swofford and the Head of School, Mr. Dillon, were waiting in the conference room. In shock and really numb, I sat down, took a deep breath, put on a smile, and went through the interview being offered a job as a Resource Teacher.

I knew they were Christians and I wanted to tell them, I wanted to reach out, I was hurting so bad, but they didn't know me personally at this point and it just wasn't the professional thing to bring up at a job interview. So, God and I, well, we made it through the final interview and then I walked to my car. I now know of course that I could have reached out to my new work family, but it just wasn't the time.

As I got to my car and sat down, I couldn't hold it back any longer. Sobs, deep heart felt cries poured out to God with tears puddling my steering wheel.

I sat in my car in that parking lot, questioning everything in my life, knowing that God was close but not understanding His purpose or His plan. My thoughts raced as I was excited that I had a new teaching position in a Christian environment, fearful of the news we just heard, not knowing if my husband was going to live or die, not sure how I could ever take care of my special needs son all by myself and more importantly how Brian would make it without Rick because they have such an amazing bond.

As I'm trying to process everything, the reality of the moment hits and I know I need to get home and love on my precious special needs son and talk with my husband so that we can try to sit and digest everything and work through the shock and numbness of this news.

When I finally had gotten myself together enough to drive up the road, my radio was on. It almost always stays tuned to 106.9, The Light, an encouraging Christian radio station in the area where we live. At this point, I'm upset, angry, frustrated, heartbroken, numb, and yet happy for my new job all at the same time. I'm so glad in the chaos of my thoughts that I didn't get pulled over by a cop. I would have been taken in as a mental case at that very second. "Shake it off, Trish", I said to myself. I took a deep breath and came back to the reality that

I'm driving subconsciously and that I really needed to be paying attention to my driving.

As my thoughts continued to race as I'm getting back to the reality of my driving, I hear the announcer on the radio announce the song, "Hallelujah, Even Here". I turned up my radio not realizing that God was about to give me the reassurance of His very Presence with me at that very moment.

Isn't it just like God, to show up in your pain and to hear your heart cries? Even in anger, frustration, desperation, and fear? So here it was, in God's words to me.... In this very song.... As the radio played......

"Hallelujah Even Here"
Lydia Laird
Verse 1-
Right now, I feel a little overwhelmed.
Right now, I could really use some help.
Right now, I don't feel like it is well with my soul.
I've tried to find a way around this mess.
I've prayed In faith that the night would end.
Right here, when I just can't understand,
I'll lift my hands.
Chorus-
Hallelujah, when the storm is relentless,
Hallelujah, when the battle is endless,
In the middle of the in between,
In the middle of the questioning,
Over every worry, every fear,
"Hallelujah Even Here."
"Hallelujah Even Here."
Verse 2-
Somehow, I bow, and my heart gets free.
Too far, too hard, becomes so easy.
I find peace here in surrendering,
In letting go,

Chorus-
Hallelujah, when the storm is relentless,
Hallelujah, when the battle is endless,
In the middle of the in between,
In the middle of the questioning,
Over every worry, every fear,
"Hallelujah Even Here."
"Hallelujah Even Here."
Bridge-
Sometimes **nothing left to give**
Ooh, becomes the **sweetest offering**
And sometimes choosing just to sing
Is the thing that changes everything.
Chorus-
Hallelujah, when the storm is relentless,
Hallelujah, when the battle is endless,
In the middle of the in between,
In the middle of the questioning,
Over every worry, every fear,
"Hallelujah Even Here."
"Hallelujah Even Here."

So, there it was. In praise, in worship, in surrender. Even in my questioning and over every worry and every fear, Hallelujah Even Here. Sobs, deep heartfelt sobs, and whispers of my heart now are puddling once again in my car as I'm heading home so much that I had to pull over for a minute to get myself together again.

I determined in my heart that day that even though God and I were having some words and to be honest with you, some weren't so very Christian like, I told my Heavenly Father that I would love Him even though I didn't understand His plan. I would lift my hands. I would praise. I would find that point of surrender that even while I still had questions, I would "Let go and Let God", as the saying goes. I would allow God to work His plan. I would trust in Him as I did when I prayed so long ago as a fifteen-year-old girl that He would heal my mom from cancer. I would TRY to find my hope and faith, even as hard as this was.

As my mind snapped back to reality once again after a time of prayer and "heart whispers" that I poured out to God, I knew I needed to get home. I knew I had to put on my brave face for my husband. I knew I needed to be strong. I needed to hold him close. Love him. Caress him.

I got home that evening. I went into our house like I normally do and scooped up my son in my arms as I always do for a hug and a kiss (yes, even at fourteen) and sang a silly jingle that he and I enjoy, but this time with even more meaning. He laughed and giggled his silly giggle and made eye contact with me leaning in for another hug. I asked him about his school day. He responded on his speech device as he is nonverbal and told me he had a happy day.

After a few minutes, I turned to my husband. And.... I just held him close. In just that moment, I kissed and embraced him like I never had before. I took in every scent of him. I felt every breath he was breathing. Life, I thought, is a vapor. It's fleeting. It's precious. I thought about all that I unintentionally take for granted each day. I just wanted to hold him .... close.... for all eternity.

Sometimes in households and daily tasks, we all get so caught up in all the agenda and the to-do lists. Sometimes hurrying around each other in between work schedules, homework, baths, supper, laundry, dishes, and sanity. Well, I thought, it's time to slow down and embrace the most important things in life. Right now, it's time to release the "what if's" and enjoy every precious moment that we are given. Right now, it's time to pray and praise, even in our unknowns, even in our uncertainty. So, in a heartbroken yet sincere spirit I cried out:

"HALLELUJAH EVEN HERE."

5

The Beginning: Our Special Needs Story

SPECIAL NEEDS FAMILIES have so much that we need to say. We have so much that we need to relate to others. We strive to educate and advocate. Families like ours have so much that need to be understood and accepted. We don't need judgement. We need love and honestly lots of it! We need prayers. We need encouragement. There are days that we are just literally trying to survive. Unless you live this life every day, it is difficult to explain. A lot of times, we make things look so easy because we know how to. Honestly, it is very, very, difficult as well emotional at times, yet the challenges never outweigh the blessings of having a special needs child.

Our special needs journey has included a multiple diagnosis of Autism, Epilepsy, Sensory Integration Dysfunction, Nonverbal Speech Apraxia, and Chromosomal Q21.1 Microdeletion Disorder. What? That's a mouthful, isn't it?

Rick and I had been married for eleven years when we found out that we were expecting. It was hilarious, but Rick detected it before I did. I remember that it was about two weeks before Thanksgiving and we were not really trying to conceive nor were we preventing it. We just figured when it was God's timing, it would happen.

It was three weeks before Thanksgiving. We always decorated for Christmas early, celebrating both Thanksgiving and Christmas together throughout the season. If you are a Christian, they kind-of go together you know when you celebrate the true meanings.

We had gotten down our Christmas decorations that weekend and were putting up our Christmas tree. We decorated it just like we always did in years past, but I just didn't like how it looked. I remember sitting down in our living room floor and crying a puddle. I kept telling Rick that it looked like a Charlie Brown Christmas Tree over and over. His laughter ensued and he came over to hold me. In between my sobs, he whispered, "Honey, I think you may be pregnant." My emotions were showing it all the way around. I laughed and said "No, I'm not!" but we both knew though that it was highly probable.

I went down to our local Walmart and bought "the test." Actually, I bought FIVE tests. I took the first one, it was positive. The second, the third, the fourth, and well the fifth and yes, they all had the same result. We laughed, we cried. We held onto each other in the excitement of the moment. We decided we were going to wait to tell our families on Thanksgiving Day.

I called the doctor to set up the appointment. The secretary laughed as I told her I had taken five tests and they were all positive. She said, "Honey, you need to come in to confirm but I would say you that we need to get you started with some prenatal vitamins as soon as possible and complete a checkup. The earliest appointment I have is for tomorrow." I made the appointment for the next day. Sure enough, Rick and I were expecting our first baby. Of course, we already knew but now we had the doctor's confirmation.

Thanksgiving Day that year was so exciting. We were going to tell our parents and our family members the news. Everyone was so ecstatic and in shock all at the same time. We had been together for so long and many thought it would never happen. I was the first born on my side and this was going to be my parents' first grandchild. Rick was the baby of his family expecting his first child. We knew our baby would be spoiled rotten, but we just didn't know how spoiled at the time!

Overall, I was blessed to have a healthy pregnancy although higher risk because of my age of thirty -two years old at the time. It was also determined early on that I had to have a Rho-Gam shot because of the RH factor, which was found, but it was treatable. No other major health issues ensued throughout the duration of my pregnancy.

I continued to work throughout my pregnancy. I really didn't have much morning sickness, although I did keep horrible allergies my whole first trimester which resulted in a major sinus infection. I had taken some over the counter Sudafed which didn't touch it. I had to end up going to the doctor to get help.

Just as all couples are when they find they are expecting, Rick and I were so extremely excited! We had waited so long and had been together literally already half of our lives having been high school sweethearts. We knew we were going to have an incredibly special child; however, at the time we literally had no idea how special he would truly be.

Months passed. I remember my work family at The Billy Graham Association where I worked in Christian Ministry at the time gathering around to pray for me. They prayed as we found out the gender. It was going to be a baby boy. We decided to name him Brian after my husband. My coworkers continued to pray for Brian's health and growth all throughout my pregnancy. It was so nice to be surrounded by Christians and those who cared and called out to God for us in our journey. We had no idea at the time just how much we would need those prayers in the days ahead for strength, wisdom, and guidance as we would be blessed with a child who had special needs.

I had a checkup with three weeks left in my pregnancy before my due date. As the doctor took measurements and examined me, he told me that I may not make it through the duration of the week, nevertheless the night. Rick and I were excited, but I wanted to make it as close to my due date as possible because the original date was going to be on our wedding anniversary.

At midnight that night, Rick kept watching me. I told him I was fine. He kept holding me tight and stroking my hair. His eyes gazed deep. He was so nervous, yet so very reserved and sweet as I told him through my laughter, to "Roll over and go to sleep." I promised him I'd be fine and wake him if I felt like I needed to go to the hospital. It's like he had a sixth sense about this night though. He fell asleep holding me so close to him that I could barely breathe, insert laughter here.

Sure enough, about 2:00 am I awoke to a gushing sound. My water had partially broken. I changed clothes and Rick grabbed the pre-packed hospital bag. We rushed to the car as I was calling our family members and told them we were on our way to the hospital. I was terrified not knowing what all to expect but knew we would be ok. All those pregnancy, training, and birthing classes were about to become a reality. I grabbed a praise and worship CD. I thought maybe if we could play it, my nerves could calm. I was a bit scared. Of course, I'd never had a baby before.

As we arrived at the hospital, my sweet son had decided by that point that he was cozy where he was and didn't want to continue to make his exit. So, my labor journey began. It was hours of walking the halls, and walking the halls, and walking the halls. Ever been there?

I should have known then that Brian was going to be strong willed and stubborn just like his parents. Between the two of us, poor Brian didn't have a chance and at the time we had no idea that we would also factor in special needs.

After about twelve hours of labor, I was getting tired. I had some pain meds at the beginning and was dilating and having contractions, but my sweet boy was not coming fast enough. After hours of walking, the doctor decided it was best to go ahead and continue by induction. I was given a round of Pitocin medication to help speed up my contractions.

It was not too long after, I was in hard labor. I remember it being the most horrible and intense pain that I had ever felt or could have ever imagined. I refused an epidural. I was afraid of the needle going in my back. I also did not get a chance to ask for other pain meds.

Brian continued to be strong-willed, but I continued to persevere as I pushed so hard to try to help my sweet boy get here. I was so tired and prayed for God to help both me and him. The nurses and doctors were great. The hospital allowed a CD player, and it was playing one of our favorite songs which seemed to calm my nerves a bit. My mom was on one side, my sister on the other, and my husband all around me, as my biggest supports in the room. Everyone was cheering us on.

I thought we would end up having to go for a Cesarean section surgery. I was so tired and just as I was about ready to just quit pushing and thought I couldn't do any more, suddenly, one last push and Brian was here! Wow, with God's help, I just had given natural birth to a miracle! I had never seen Rick's face so lit up. He was already such a proud daddy! It warmed my heart to see him so ecstatic. Rick cut the umbilical cord and watched Brian as he got his first bath while the nurses had some things to finish with me.

Even with all the pain, when I held Brian, I knew he was worth it. Worth all the intense pain- Worth all the time I had been waiting to see him and to hold him. He was angelic. He was beautiful. Rick and I knew that God had created this miracle through us and that he was our very own special gift from God.

6

Adjusting with Early Sickness and Emotional Strain

GETTING HOME FROM the hospital and bringing in our sweet baby boy was one memory that I will forever hold in my heart. It was us. Our sweet new little family. Rick and I already had such a close and strong relationship, but now, to bring this sweet little boy into our home made us both feel so complete.

Brian was so tiny having been born three weeks early. His little fingers and smacking lips were so sweet. He was so precious, and I just couldn't stop looking at him. He had webbed toes on both of his feet which were called swimmer's feet of which we really were not concerned with at the time because the doctor had said that there were tons of children born with webbed toes and unless it affected his walking or mobility, we should not worry about it immediately. We would eventually find out, though, many years later, that this was a trait of his rare genetic chromosome micro-deletion disorder, 1Q21.1.

The first week with our little fella was a big adjustment to say the least! We only thought we didn't get to sleep before we had kids. Boy, were we in for a huge surprise as we had a boy who didn't like to sleep! It was very exhausting that first little bit as we tried to juggle our responsibilities with lack of sleep and being new parents, but thankfully with teamwork and determination, we made it all work together. As my maternity leave ticked away, I was grateful for every minute that I had with our sweet new baby boy. As I basked in joy with each new day, I was in awe of him. It was us, our little family of three learning to adjust and really learning about life and just how very much we truly loved each other.

As the weeks went on, we noticed that Brian seemed to be increasingly and progressively fussy. Some told us he was considered a colicky baby. We found out that he had some gastrological issues and milk allergies of which he would eventually thankfully outgrow.

Rick and I loved Brian so much. We did not realize that we had a child with special needs as we would find out in time and that his needs were more neurological and cognitive in nature and would take a great deal of love and patience to sort through.

At the time, we were just not sure what was happening as Brian did not seem to like a lot of snuggles and cuddles and would rare back and scream with these horrible fits. I really can't describe it. Unless you've experienced it, it's unlike anything I had ever seen.

These "fits" were like a nightmare or even many nightmares all at once. The doctor's deemed it as "night terrors." No matter what was done, nothing seemed to soothe and neither could he seem to self-soothe. At the time we didn't know about the sensory issues and the self-regulation issues that were of course attributed to autism.

Through tears, heartbreak, and confusion, we continued to try to love on Brian and cuddle him, of course trying swaddling, walking, bouncing, rocking, holding him tight, kissing him, singing, and looking for signs of what may be wrong, but not understanding all the "whys" or the "hows."

We continued to enamor him with all the attention and love that we could give him. We would learn later that he would eventually grow to understand this affection and that he would learn to love and reciprocate this love in such amazing ways. Looking at my sweet boy now, I am so thankful that we didn't give up and kept doing all the right things even when we felt the hope"less"ness in our situation as parents.

It was in the wee hours of the night one night that I was questioning everything and crying out to God. I was sad, heartbroken, and frustrated. Exhaustion had set in for both me and Rick. He was also trying to figure all of this out and wanted to love Brian with everything within him and be the best dad for his son. The hardest thing in the world as a parent is to not be able to help. No matter what we did, it just seemed to be a never-ending battle of tears, frustration, and stress. We just couldn't fix it.

"OK, God,"
"I Need You!"
"Help Us!"

We were both exhausted, but we remembered the Praise and Worship music CD that we played in the hospital. Frantically, we put the CD in and miraculously Brian calmed down that night with the same songs he heard as he entered the world.

Finally, after hours of Brian's screams, it was silence, it was quiet. Dead silence as we turned off the music when he fell asleep in my arms. My head was splitting with a headache. As I watched my baby boy drift off to sleep, I was so heartbroken and feeling so helpless as a mom and I felt like a failure because I just could not seem to make everything right. That's what a mom is supposed to do. Fix it. It seemed no matter how hard I tried; nothing was working.

Brian had literally screamed himself to sleep in my arms against my chest night after night while I was holding him and rocking him. I had tried everything I knew. The music seemed to calm him down at times. As time went on, I would question myself, wondering why I couldn't seem to help soothe my very own son as I felt like I was failing as a mom. I would call my mom crying and asking for advice. I wanted to find out what I could do differently to help him-anything at all- I was so desperate.

I was questioning everything and felt helpless. Maybe I just wasn't cut out for this mothering thing. I was thirty-two years old and felt like

I didn't have a clue at how to be a mother! It didn't seem as simple as I thought it was going to be. Those parenting magazines and all the advice I had been given as well as knowing what to do to help a typical child wasn't working. I just didn't understand. Heartbroken and frustrated, I felt helpless. As I sobbed on my husband's shoulders and he held me close, I remember telling him that I didn't know if I could do this.

Rick and I would hold onto each other with tears during these times trying to figure it all out. I just wanted to know what we were doing wrong. It just didn't seem fair that we were working so hard to be good parents but could not seem to soothe this precious boy of which we loved more than anything in the world.

My mom was a great mom and had taught me so much. I loved babies. I had also helped to take care of my brother and sister so many times helping my mom and dad, as my parents had struggled on and off with sickness, so I knew that I was capable. I had helped with babies in the church nursery; however, at this point in my life, I felt like such a failure and didn't understand completely why I couldn't help my very own child.

Little did Rick and I realize that it wasn't our fault; nor was it our precious baby boy as he couldn't help it either. He had autism and seizures that were plaguing his mind as well as sensory issues of which we knew absolutely nothing about at the time.

One day when I was at work, my mom discovered Brian had a tongue tie that the doctor's office did not catch upon his newborn evaluation, but thankfully, it was mild and still found early. Brian was scheduled for surgery to free his tongue tie which helped at the time with his feeding challenges.

Brian also had a history of ear infections and croup episodes. He struggled a lot with these issues early on and we found ourselves in the doctor's office every few weeks. It was so frustrating at the time. We would continue to try to relieve his symptoms from suggestions of raising the head of the bed, using a cool mist humidifier as well as a nebulizer with albuterol and a lot of times ended up with steroids as well to help clear his airways.

At times I would just lean over Brian's crib after laying him down to make sure he was still breathing. One night Brian was struggling to breathe and turning blue when he was around six months old and seemed to be coughing with every other breath. We ended up taking a ride in an ambulance to the Levine's Children Hospital in Charlotte where Brian was admitted and given rounds of strong steroids and breathing treatments. Over time, thankfully, he has outgrown these croup/asthmatic style episodes. Even as Brian grows as a teenager, I still check on him consistently, even at nighttime. There is just something about a special needs parent's heart that will always have that little bit of fear and concern when there is this type of issue.

7

Early Signs of Autism and Epilepsy

As time progressed, Brian was delayed in meeting a good many of his milestones. Boys are sometimes more delayed than girls as infants and toddlers, so we thought that maybe he was just running a little behind.

Early on, we noticed that Brian would stare off on occasion and didn't smile very much at first. It appeared to be blank stares and we had no idea at the time, but Brian was having silent seizures attributed to Epilepsy in addition to Autism.

Brian would line up his toys from the smallest to the largest from around three months old to around six months old which was both amazing yet strange. Brian loved to watch things spin, especially his mobile, but all infants did this so we did not really think much of it until we noticed he would watch the ceiling fan spin around and around and move his eyes with the spinning, almost like an obsessive-compulsive trait. It is very evident when we watch our older home videos although at the time we really didn't know or really understand that this was a characteristic trait of Autism.

Developmentally, Brian rolled over around the desired time. We noticed early on that he had a sensitive gag reflux which we attributed to his tongue tie; however, we did find out later that his gag reflux was actually because of oral texture sensitivity to foods which again is also a sensory challenge associated with Autism.

Once Brian started to walk, (he walked before he crawled), we noticed that after lining up his toys, he would spin around and around and then flap his hands. He also flapped his hands when he was excited or happy. He would scan items and did not play appropriately with his toys. He seemed to be more interested in the functions of his toys, such as watching the wheels on his car spin instead of making the car roll back and forth as it was intended to do.

Brian loved to watch various clips of movies, trailers, logos, and listen to parts of music instead of watching or listening to them in completion at times. Later, we would also find out, this was a "stim", also known as "self-stimulatory" behavior attributed to Autism.

Sometimes people with Autism have more "noticeable" stims which can make them look peculiar or odd such as rocking back and forth or hand flapping. In all actuality, their brains work so differently and sometimes they are either anxious and dealing with their anxiety or happy and expressing it outwardly but just in a different way than we do. Come on, admit it, you know you have smacked gum, tapped pencils, clicked pens, popped your knuckles, and fidgeted around, all because you were excited, had nervous energy, or just needed to move. That, my friends, is what stimming looks like in a typical individual.

Moving on to transitions…. Oh boy! I remember back how the episodes of screaming worsened and as we had to transition from one activity or place to the next one the screaming became horrific. Man, the stares we got. Going out in public was hard. We never knew what may trigger Brian to get upset, we just continued to do all that we knew to try to help him. We didn't give up. We just kept trying. Sometimes people were sympathetic, sometimes judgmental, and sometimes our worst nightmare. We tried our best to both soothe and/or discipline, if necessary, but a lot of times these situations were struggles that Brian couldn't help. We didn't want others to think we were horrible parents or were raising what they assumed was a "bratty" child, but at times, honestly, people's assumptions killed my heart as they truly didn't understand what we were going through.

I think back and remember that going out to eat was a joke. We would get in and order our meal, but by the time the food arrived we would be asking for "to go" boxes because Brian would scream. A walk around the mall we thought would be fun with Brian in his stroller. That was a nightmare. Little did we know at the time that it was because of over-stimulation with lights that were too bright. Amusement parks, with noise levels that were too loud, oh boy! Sensitivity to sights and sounds that were also huge signs of sensory processing disorder which are also related to Autism of which we had no idea.

Going to church, well we tried. It was even harder in the early years. I would usually end up in the nursery because Brian would usually get so upset that we would have to eventually leave and just go home.

It was during these times that I felt so defeated. I would look around at other moms and their kids and think what is wrong with me? I would blame myself for not being "good" enough and not being able to help my son. Now that I look back, I knew in my heart there had to be some answers to this, somewhere. I just couldn't seem to grasp what was happening and didn't understand anything about it at the time. But, regardless, I knew I loved him. He was my heart and I'd do anything in my power to help him.

As time progressed, Brian's speech was severely delayed. At first, of course, we attributed this to his tongue tie. He started babbling and we could hear the sound, ma, ma, ma, ma, but it didn't progress much, it wasn't consistent, and it eventually stopped.

We didn't know at the time that Brian would eventually be diagnosed with speech delays attributed to Autism resulting not only in a delay of speech, but also, he would be considered "non-verbal" with Speech Apraxia being a contributing factor. As a mom, it was so hard to hear that my son may never speak. So many take that for granted. My advice: Always listen to your children and never ever take their words for granted. Some parents would give anything just to hear a "chatter box" for any length of time.

My mom and my sister (being an Early Childhood major), as well as Rick's mom were all instrumental in helping us pick up on Brian's delays. By twelve months old, Brian was still not talking, and his babbling had stopped. He still made sounds, but it wasn't considered functional speech even though he could hum tunes or say things in his mind and hum it out, it would only come out as sounds as he couldn't make his mouth and his brain work together to produce the words.

We made the decision to talk with our pediatrician about all that we were seeing. We were not sure where all of this would lead, but we decided it was time to explore some options to find out what may be going on. It was difficult to think that there may be something that was a developmental issue or a neurological and cognitive issue, but we knew we needed help and we wanted to help Brian any way we could, so we sought out professional advice.

8

First steps to Diagnosis-Developmental Delays and Early Intervention

WE TOOK THE first step of talking with Brian's pediatrician at twelve months old, thinking that maybe there may be some issues that we needed to explore further. At first, to be very honest, the pediatrician that we had at the time wasn't very helpful at all, so we went to a new doctor for a second opinion.

We received a referral from the doctor's office for BABYNET, a state agency in our state that helps provide services for delays in infants and toddlers. Brian had a few evaluations and these assessments helped us confirm delays and become eligible to receive Early Intervention. As Brian turned fourteen months old, we started with an Early Interventionist named Ashleigh from Easter Seals coming out to our house to help us work on evaluations and goals to help us understand the challenges that we were seeing and to engage Brian with new techniques to try.

We were blessed with two great Early Interventionists, Ashleigh and Robin, which would both, in turn, become friends. They didn't judge me as a mom, and it felt so good to have someone to help me understand and calm my fears. They saw how dedicated I was to Brian and how much I wanted to help him. I was so desperate during those times but knew we would be okay.

Early on, Ashleigh had a contagious spirit. She came in and her care and enthusiasm helped me to deal with all that was happening. She was always positive. As Brian's first Early Interventionist, she was instrumental in helping me get started on the journey to an evaluation for Autism and a diagnosis which forever changed our lives.

The Early Intervention goals that we worked on were always introduced in fun and exciting ways. I grew to not only enjoy having Brian's *Early Interventionist* come to visit, but Brian did also. Although we had plenty of work cut out for us, I was so grateful to have someone that could relate to the things that we were going through and bring a breath of fresh air.

One day Ashleigh mentioned that it appeared that there could be "traits" of Autism. I looked at her and said, "Ashleigh, what is that?" She comforted me and told me that it was a disorder that required a medical diagnosis but that there was help. So, of course, after she left and I finally was able to get Brian settled down for a nap, I did what any plugged-in parent would do. I started research. At fourteen-months old, Brian had a lot of traits of Autism. Why didn't I know about this? I googled and researched Autism and everything I could think of that would be related.

And then...
It hit me.
"Autism."

Those "Whispers of my Heart" engulfed me as I began crying puddles of tears. As I sat alone and sobbed, my hot wet tears streamed down my face and for the first time, I thought that we may have finally found some answers to some of what had been happening, although my heart was broken. When Rick got his break at work and called me,

I explained to him that we would be seeing some specialists to help us in our near future. Relieved but not knowing what to expect, we were both ready to get help for our sweet boy.

Since Brian didn't respond to his name or make eye contact when we called his name, my husband and I had also thought that maybe there were some problems with Brian's hearing as well. Little did we realize that a child not responding to their name is also a sign of Autism. A good bit of the time Brian also appeared "locked in his own world."

We set up an appointment with a pediatric eye, ear, nose, and throat doctor and was referred to an Audiologist. After a battery of sound booth testing that Brian did respond to but inconsistently, it was decided that Brian needed to have a BAER test (better known as a Brainstem Auditory Evoked Response) test to check the level of his hearing. This test is an electro-diagnostic hearing test used to evaluate brainwaves for sounds. The procedure looked scarier than it was. Brian was hooked up to electrodes and put to sleep to check his hearing and brainwave response. Brian's hearing was perfect.

We continued to explore our next steps with Autism, what we could expect as far as diagnosis and treatment, as well as learning everything that we could about the things that were happening. I had no idea that we would be a special needs family, but here we were, starting this journey that we absolutely knew nothing about, but would learn in time from the best teacher that God could have ever given us, our very own son.

9

Autism Diagnosis and Speech Therapy

WE WERE GIVEN a lot of information from the doctors and honestly, I was feeling a bit overwhelmed as I was trying to wrap my mind around everything. We had changed pediatricians at this point and had Brian's records transferred so we felt very comfortable discussing our findings with Brian's new pediatrician, Dr. Hansen.

Dr. Hansen was so helpful as he confirmed delays and agreed about the autistic traits. A referral to a Developmental Pediatrician, a doctor who specialized in Autism, was suggested as well as a Psychological Evaluation. We sought out a reputable Developmental Pediatrician who was referred to us from my cousin's wife, Amy, who knew about our situation and who also had a daughter who had been diagnosed with a milder form of Autism. Dr. Stegman was also a part of our healthcare system and Dr. Hansen also highly recommended him, so we knew we had finally found a team of professionals to help.

The developmental appointment was booked ten months out. It was going to be a long ten months before Brian would officially be seen by Dr. Stegman because at the time Autism seemed to be taking off like a jet plane as so many children were being diagnosed during this time. Dr. Stegman was one of the best doctors in the area and I

was so excited to know that we were finally going to have some answers as light slowly started protruding through our darkness.

During this time of waiting, we continued with Early Intervention,
pursued a speech assessment along with a psychological evaluation,
and took every step we knew of to get the ball rolling with this new-
found highly expected diagnosis.

The assessments at the speech center that we were referred to, of
course, as we knew, resulted in a severe delay in speech. It is so hard
to hear on a normal basis that your child may never speak and will be
considered "non-verbal". We understood. We got it; we really did. We
really needed help, guidance, and reassurance at this point.

Let's just say that our first encounter with a private speech pathologist was not a very positive or intriguing experience. With a lack of
professionalism, this speech pathologist had a very "dry personality"
to say the least. She also did not have a very compassionate spirit. I'm
sure she was just trying to be realistic with us, but her unprofessional
approach is one that I will never forget.

To hear from someone that is considered a professional that your
child will never be able to show or reciprocate the love that you expect
and that as a couple you may want to consider having another child or
use adoption as another option hurt my heart in unimaginable ways.
This was strictly her opinion, but it still radiates in my head to this very
day. How unprofessional and how wrong she was! Now understanding Autism, I do understand some of what she was trying to portray to
us as parents, but because of the lack of concern and unprofessional-
ism, we sought out a second opinion. My mama-bear came out that
day and I refused to believe that my son would not be capable of love.

A **"dis"**ability can become a differing **"ABILITY."** In my heart I
know that I have pushed so hard to help Brian and prove that with
God all things are possible. You would be amazed at how much Brian
can show you. Brian has learned to not only communicate with his
diagnosis of Speech Apraxia, but he also loves so big and reciprocates
that love to others in more ways than anyone could have ever imagined. We give the credit to God and we also give ourselves a good bit

of credit as a mom and dad who just don't give up during the hard times and knew our son could do more than what we were told.

Ten long months had passed and finally on October 9, 2009, we received a diagnosis of Autism and Sensory Integration Dysfunction for Brian which would forever change our lives. We knew, but to have it on paper validated it for us. Even though we knew the diagnosis was highly probable, I still cried.

On the way home, I was a bundle of nerves, but also felt that we finally had the answers we needed. I also needed to be sure that my husband was ok. He had been a strong support and he and I were in this together. I knew that in my heart, but I needed to hear his thoughts. I asked Rick, "Honey, we've been together for a long time. Are you sure that you will be ok with this?" I needed to know. I knew my husband. I knew that he loved us. I just needed his reassurance.

This news would mean that with his delays, Brian would be more dependent than independent as we had already noticed. He would continue to be delayed and would learn, grow, and progress much slower and differently than others. We would need to pour a lot of our time and effort into his progression and have more patience than ever imagined. This would change our dreams and our future as well.

With tears in his eyes, he assured me. He said "Trish, I love God, I love you, and I love Brian. I promise I will be here. I'm not going any- where." Then, with tears in his eyes, he proceeded to sing me a song by Steven Curtis Chapman- "I Will Be Here," and I knew he meant every word.

Insert crying face here. Over the years my husband has proven this over and over and time and time again. I know no matter what we may face, even now throughout his cancer diagnosis, he will always be here, and we will always be together... for now, and for all eternity, whether in this earthly life that we live or ultimately in Heaven.

10

Occupational Therapy and Self-Regulation

ONCE WE RECEIVED the Autism diagnosis, it was time to search out an Occupational Therapist to help with the sensory challenges. I will never forget the two exceptional private Occupational Therapists that we were blessed to have, Keira and Meghan. They taught us so very much about Brian and his sensory system with both vestibular input and proprioceptive input. If you don't know about your body's sensory input system, you may find this very interesting.

Proprioceptive input is the sense through which our body perceives position and movement, while Vestibular input is the receiving of information regarding our body's movement in space in relation to our head movements sending signals to the brain.

Individual with Autism sometimes can't make sense of these sensory systems and need help to regulate and control their bodies, almost like they don't know their "personal space," at times. Occupational Therapists can help with this type of input by providing activities and techniques that help to enhance awareness of the body as well as strengthen weak muscles and motor skills. They also have techniques to help with texture sensitivities as these challenges can also affect individuals with an Autism diagnosis.

I thought it was crazy insane at first, until I watched my son in a therapy session. The OT introduced a weighted vest, a weighted blanket, sensory swings, and many other different therapy tools that actually enhanced Brian's learning. He would work super hard and seemed to focus more when he had input that helped both his vestibular and proprioceptive systems. Tactile awareness also was a huge struggle, but with time and patience, they also helped to guide us on how to help with this as well as Brian's oral texture sensitivity and weak motor skills that were attributed to Autism.

We still use sensory strategies at times to help Brian as well as a chew tube that helps him with anxiety and a sensory chew necklace to chew on when he becomes angry to help him fuel his anger in a healthy way. I was amazed that these sorts of techniques could help, but they did. Essential oils also helped with anxiety as well and provided some additional support with mood and self-regulation. I am a firm believer in Occupational Therapy as I have watched and am amazed at how techniques used can aide with awareness and learning. If you are questioning, Occupational Therapy is an amazing therapy and support for individuals with special needs.

11

Applied Behavioral Therapy and Early Special Needs School Services

AS TIME PROGRESSED, we became involved with ABA therapy, also known as Applied Behavioral Analysis Therapy. We learned so much about helping Brian adjust to real-life situations and academic situations by using techniques from Applied Behavioral Analysis Therapy which encourages performance based on positive reinforcement techniques while understanding the functions of behavior and how to best handle varying behaviors that children with Autism can exhibit.

Brian had two amazing private BCBA's (Board Certified Behavioral Analysts) named Sarah and Spencer, and some really great line therapists, Jessica, Michelle, and Kelly, beginning at two and a half years old in a private therapy program. I never will forget all that Sarah, Michelle, Kelly, and Jessica did to help with Brian and his needs as well as become good friends to our family. We all learned about Brian and how to help him together. Michelle, Kelly, and Jessica were with me through some really tough days. I'm so thankful they were there to offer support and help.

As I remember certain triggers for Brian and self-regulation challenges, I think back to one day that I will never forget. Brian was afraid of loud noises in particularly, sirens. Sirens, however, are so important to daily life and Brian needed to know that if he heard sirens, help was on the way, whether it was a police officer, a firetruck, or an ambulance. Every time we would hear or pass sirens when out and about, even in our car, Brian would scream these horrific screams and become so upset. It took so long to get him calmed down even on a normal day out and about in these types of situations.

One day while Rick was at work, we had therapy. I knew it was going to be a difficult day. I knew Brian would scream and cup his ears. I knew it was going to be hard to put him through a round of "hearing sirens" but I knew that we had to get him adjusted to some real-life situations to help him learn how to tolerate them. You can't live in the world unless you can tolerate things around you. I knew what we had to do, but I was terrified. I knew we were about to be on "meltdown alert."

Michelle and Jessica (Brian's therapists at the time) and I had planned an outing for his therapy session that day. We were going to a "Firetruck Fun Day" at the Boyd Hill Community Center with Kinder- Arc, a wonderful program in our area that helps children with disabilities have "structure and fun educational play" during the summer. It is usually organized by Terry, a wonderful woman and advocate who is the Recreation Leader at the City of Rock Hill. She has been a constant for many years now helping with special needs families as well as many special needs events including The Special Olympics in our area and now the local new inclusive playground in our area for special needs, "Miracle Park."

Michelle, Brian, and I arrived at the Friday fun day. Immediately Brian began screaming because he saw a fire truck and he knew the fire truck was going to be loud. It was so hard to get him out of his car seat and get him past the fire truck inside to the other fun activities in full meltdown mode.... but we did it.

As it was time for the Firemen to let the kids get in the truck, hit the buttons, flash the sirens, and spray the hose, I knew we had to get

Brian out there to conquer this fear. I knew he would hate it, at first. I knew it would be hard to put him through it, yet with Michelle's help, I knew if we could help him with the noise levels and help him see what fun a fire truck could be as well as understand how they help us, maybe we could conquer this.

It was a disaster, well at first. Brian could tolerate the noise for a few seconds and then he would scream. We just kept trying by bringing him in and out for longer periods each time until he got used to some of the noise level and actually tolerated it for just a little bit longer each time and then we would immediately reinforce him with something he enjoyed. We would rush inside before meltdown mode and give him time to diffuse. Then, yep, it was back at it, building up his tolerance to the noise, allowing him to see how fun it could be, and helping with adjustment to the noise levels by helping him cover his ears.

Patience and persistence paid off. Brian actually started enjoying the day. He was having fun at the fire truck. He got to wear a fireman's hat. He actually, "SMILED!" He got rewarded on the way home with his favorite, "McDonald's!"

I learned ALOT that day. Things were going to be tough as we had already experienced. Real life situations that a lot take for granted, could turn our world upside down in just a few seconds. I learned that Brian could be taught and helped to adjust to things that at times were necessary which at times I thought would be impossible, yet knew we had to follow through to help him.

He still has things that he doesn't like. No, I don't make him adjust to everything that he hates. We all have our likes and dislikes. Sometimes, though, we must conquer certain things in life that will help us in situations of normal everyday life and circumstances. I knew in my heart that Brian could learn. He had to learn that these kind community service workers were here to help us.

I can tell you that as hard as this adjustment period was to conquer, to this day, Brian loves firetrucks even his own that he plays with here at home. Every time one passes us now, whether a firetruck, ambulance, or police officer, Brian smiles. We stop and pray, "Jesus, help them as they help someone else." Brian now gets it, he truly does.

Throughout the duration of private ABA therapy even up until our present day at fourteen-years-old now, I can never speak enough of Kelly, another one of Brian's "girlfriend" therapists. He truly had a crush on this beautiful friend who also loved Brian. We told Brian that he wasn't allowed to date older women, just kidding. Kelly was phenomenal. Brian made so much progress with Kelly as she had mannerisms that were kind and gentle, just like his mama, yet pushed him when needed. She knew that he loved logos. He loved to scroll (and still does) movie logos such as "20th Century Fox, PBS Kids, etc. Kelly would have Brian complete his work and then he would get rewarded with his logos. She even made him a laminated logo book and he could ask for this on his speech iPad. Kelly and her positivity will forever be one of my very best memories as she helped my son "breakthrough" some of his Autism in such a mothering way.

We were also blessed just a few months after Brian turned two to have a home visit and be evaluated by two great school psychologists, Angela and Sarah who placed us in an Applied Behavioral Therapy program offered by our local school district. At just three years old, Brian started this amazing program where we would also have a School Supported BCBA (Mrs. Revels), and Lead Teacher (Mrs. Sims) along with three great ABA therapists (Mrs. Dorsey, Mrs. Gore, and Mrs. Faulkner at the time).

Mrs. Dorsey, who was his first school therapist and teacher, would help Brian soothe for his midday nap while at school in the program that he attended for seven hours a day at just three years old. She would always help him by rubbing or scratching the palm of his hands as I did for him to soothe to go to sleep. It was a comfort to know that she took care of him in my absence until school was over. She gave us goals, advice, and tips to work on at home that helped tremendously. I will always remember Mrs. Dorsey as Brian's very first "teacher mama."

The next school year, Brian was blessed with Mrs. Gore, a therapist who loved Brian so much. One day I will never ever forget was the time I went to pick Brian up and he came running to me for a huge hug and made eye contact all the way to me as I scooped him up in my arms. That was the first time he came running towards me as if to say, "MOM, I LOVE YOU! I SEE YOU! I WANT TO BE WITH YOU!" "LET'S GO HOME!" Leslie and I cried together, and I hugged her so tight. I was so happy to see that breakthroughs were being made!

Ms. Faulkner, another therapist in Brian's third year of the school Early Intervention program, saw Brian's potential and she would tell me just how smart he was. I knew it of course, but to hear it from other people sure gave us a boost. She knew we were parents that followed through with Brian and she would send home extra things for us to try to tackle. She bought Brian the book "Oh, The Places You Will Go," by Dr. Suess. Never in a million years would I have thought we would be where we are. But she was right, and God still isn't finished with Brian yet. He is still learning and growing daily, and we will be as successful as we can possibly be and continue to strive to meet goals with each day that passes.

I can never speak enough about this Autism program that not only helped my son, but also helped our family with income, as I would eventually work in this program with training as an ABA therapist to help other kids just like my sweet Brian and would work with therapists that had Brian's best interest at heart as we would celebrate each victory that was made. In addition to Brian's therapists and many teachers who were so dedicated to the cause, I also made many life-long friends in my time in the classrooms at York Schools, Beverly, Vicki, Amber, Michelle, Laura, Courtney, Sierra, Catherine, Cara, Sherry, Kari, Ashley, Mandy, Jennifer C., Jennifer H., Mary, Connie, Sheri, and Anna.

Thankfully, in addition to private OT and speech, we were blessed with amazing school professionals, Judy, Nancy, Andrea, and Wendy, throughout the duration of elementary school and parts of middle school. Andrea was so great as she helped Brian with sensory needs in the school setting and had tons of suggestions to help throughout his school days. Nancy will always hold a special place in my heart as well as she was such an encouragement and motivated Brian to use his words even on days when he didn't want to and continues to be a friend of mine to this very day. I will forever be grateful to her and her knowledge of speech therapy as well as Wendy, who helped push Brian to succeed.

We now have continued ABA therapy services on a case monitor basis as needed, with a great private team, including BCBA's and therapists who continue to reach out and help us as we continue programs to help Brian succeed in his older years as he matures and grows. No longer do we have extensive therapy since those horrific meltdowns have decreased greatly over the years. We have learned so much that has helped Brian become successful. At this point, there aren't many things that we can't enjoy. We have a blast now out in the community as well as church settings as a family and Brian has thrived in more ways than we could have ever imagined possible.

Brian also had many teachers that helped him throughout our continued duration of time in school. Mrs. Blackwelder, Mrs. Hill, Mrs. Timmons, and Mrs. Clemence. These four teachers helped Brian in so many ways and some even spoiled that kid completely rotten! I will never ever take for granted the time and effort poured into Brian by these teachers as well as these assistants in particular: Mrs. Theriot, Mrs. Jenner, Mrs. Trent, Mrs. Templeton, Mrs. Gill, Mrs. Cook, Mrs. Dee, Mrs. Pharr, Mrs. Godfrey, Mrs. Ward, Mrs. Shaver, Mrs. Noe, and Mrs. Washington, as well as Mrs. Crawford, nor will I forget the love of his bus drivers, Ms. Kelly and Ms. Sara who helped me on days when I would have to put that little fella on the bus to be transported to a different school.

It's amazing how you not only learn from professionals who are there to help, but you become so grateful to be blessed with others who want to help. There are times, however, when you also learn to advocate for your child and find a common ground to make it all work together. All special needs children are different. Sometimes, even though common protocols and procedures are put in place and are used to teach, it takes tweaking to find the right approach and personality traits to work together as factors in how the child learns. It's important to match personality traits with those that will work well with the individual child as well as look at the child's needs or triggers of behavior.

Although this professional help is a lot of times very significant and beneficial, it hasn't always been ideal and at times as Brian's parents, on more than one occasion, Rick and I have both had to speak up and speak out to be Brian's "voice", in both private and school settings. We had some disagreements at times on the best ways to make it all work together for Brian's benefit, but everyone on our team truly had Brian's best interest at heart.

Rick and I both are still very receptive to professional opinions, help, and protocols; however, at various times we've had to advocate for him when the programs have been too much or too intensive. It's also important to note that although a child may not be able to "vocalize", as most individuals do, they can still understand, see, feel, hear, and have emotions and feelings. You don't have to be a bully to get your point across to them.

We have always made sure to attend every IEP (Individualized Education Program) meeting to advocate and work together with our private therapists and school therapists to ensure that Brian's goals and needs are being met both at home and at school. Although there are a lot of really great Special Education Teachers and Therapists, there are also times when the book knowledge cannot even come close to being compared to the real-life experiences of a parent's twenty-four-hour day. There are times when advocacy for your child and your situation becomes a necessity for others to truly understand.

Now into his high school years, Brian is thriving and progressing daily in a homeschool program with parent administration as Rick and I both homeschool in between our work scheduling with a self-home-based curriculum including, but not limited to, academics, socialization, and self-help skills as well as continued private therapy-based services. We also utilize State Coordination services based on help and services through The Department of Disabilities and Special Needs with a Job Vocational Rehab and Coaching option as Brian gets a bit older with two great coordinators, Alyssa and Deandre.

12

How can a Non-verbal Child Communicate?

BRIAN IS CONSIDERED by professionals to be "non-verbal". As a mom and an advocate for my son, I strongly disagree with this term although I understand that the term is used because Brian can't "vocalize" his words with Speech Apraxia being the contributing factor. He can make sounds and imitate sounds as well as hum tunes to music and phrases that he enjoys which amazes everyone who hears him, but those words? Well, they just can't connect from his brain to his mouth.

As mentioned previously, Brian was not talking within normal milestone range nor was he able to communicate functionally. When he was around twelve to fourteen months old, he started to babble, but that completely stopped.

We started to teach some sign language and Brian began to learn a few basic signs. It was, however, more difficult for him with his fine motor challenges so we started with a communication system called "PECS" once we were introduced into the school program. As we were introduced to "PECS" (acronym for Picture Exchange Communication System), we were amazed that Brian was such a visual leaner and could learn through pictures. This was a great start since Brian was a visual learner and this program used visual pictures to help with communication.

The PECS system is used widely with kids with Autism, and it taught a form of communication which utilized pictures in exchange for the requested item or activity. The idea is for the individual to give a picture to another recipient to receive what is asked for.

We started with this PECS system that our school district introduced and then as time progressed our private speech therapist, Andrea, as well as our private BCBA therapist, Sarah, both introduced us to an iPad program called "ProLoQuo2Go, an awesome program that uses a "PECS" style system. We decided to personally purchase this app and bought an iPad to install it. We were amazed to realize that we had a "tech savvy" son who would learn so much through this program.

The app was costly, around $200.00 to purchase, but this program has been one of the best purchases that we have ever made! It is a communication app that includes features where real pictures of items can be taken and typed in to label the items and give a computerized voice. This system gave Brian a spoken "voice" as well as being able to type out his wants and/or needs to communicate!

Other great features of "ProLoQuo2Go" includes a spelling/typing keyboard as well as a QWERTY keyboard which enables the user to learn how to type and spell words as well as sentences to aide in answering questions as well and making requests. I am a firm believer in Adaptive Communication as we have seen and lived the benefits of this type of communication! So…. Yes, this is a huge plug for the Adaptive Communication Business, especially the program, ProLoQuo2Go. I cannot imagine where we would be if we had not purchased this as an option to help our son communicate as well as answer questions and type.

Andrea, Brian's speech therapist from Chit-Chat Speech and Language Therapy has been amazing utilizing this program as well as Brian teaching her when he has figured out things that she didn't know that he could say or do with this program.

We have used this system with my son since he was five and a half years old. Now at fourteen years old he can blow you away with the things that he can communicate to you as well as type. At first, it wasn't readily accepted in the school system, but now iPad communication is used almost indefinitely with varying programs as technology has exploded with programs like this for communication purposes. We know that we made the right choice for Brian and continue to help him thrive.

We have stored items in folders as well on Brian's speech system including our vacation locations, household items, school folders, movies, books, toys, places to eat, stores, malls, church activities as well as anything you can think of to help Brian communicate and understand in his way to make conversation and have communication. We take this "voice" everywhere we go, and Brian uses it religiously. This program has completely changed Brian from "nonverbal" to very much having a lot of things to tell us all!

Brian can introduce himself, tell you his birthday, his age, who his parents are, where he lives, his phone number and communicate various conversations that are vital to help us understand his wants and needs as well as provide others with a sense of back-and-forth conversation when interacting with Brian.

Although there are still deficits at times when things may not be as concrete as needed, and at times updates are needed, my son can still maneuver this app like the back of his hand. He can request food, ask to go to the bathroom, tell us items he wants to play with, as well as answer academic and comprehensive questions on his level. What is amazing is his most recent knowledge of adding his own items and/or activities or tying things out to communicate with others which he has continued to learn proficiently.

Brian has a voice. He uses a variety of methods to communicate and get his points across. He uses his physical voice with enunciations and vocalizations to sing songs or hum tunes or jingles. He uses his gestures or signs that he still remembers on occasion. He uses his speech app, to say or type out words or phrases, answer questions, and tact and label items. He gives high fives, hugs, and smiles, forms of "non" verbal communication, yet so clearly understood.

God has always known how much that Brian knew in his mind but couldn't get out through his words. There can be a "verbal" to a "non"verbal. If you listen closely to a non-verbal individual, you will hear the language of love that comes from the heart. Sometimes, love truly needs no spoken words! God has proven through my son that miracles do still indeed happen------every single day! We, of course, wait to hear spoken words, hoping that one day it will happen. He has been able to voice "mama" on occasion as well as one time a very brief "Elmo," but without consistency and continuation. Again, we know that when words don't come easily, Brian will continue to speak the love of language from his heart.

13

The Dreaded Medication Conversation

MEDICATION CAN BE a dreaded topic of conversation for special needs parents, and at times, let me just say that medication can be pushed too much. I have become an advocate for specific types of meds, but not without a lot of consideration, prayer, and tears with a lot of trial and error. Medication can help to treat symptoms when the right mix of meds and therapy are used, but it can be a bumpy road and needs a lot of prayer, patience, and good decision-making skills when considering. Yes, medication is helpful and recommended by both my husband and me, but finding the right mix of meds can be difficult..

I will share with you both our horror stories as well as our success stories involving the use of medication for Brian's needs. When considering medication for certain illnesses, God gives us common sense. He can heal illness, or if He chooses to, He can use doctors and nurses along with medication to help with certain medical needs.

With Autism and other related neurological and hyperactivity disorders, there are medications that can be prescribed to help with clarity and focus as well as mood swings. Epilepsy also involves the use of medication to help control seizures. Medication choices should be a very personal decision and I highly recommend considering all factors including side effects when talking with the doctor.

Trial and error of medications can be tricky and is not an easy path to maneuver as you know if you have any illness that requires medication. I'll share with you how our journey first began with meds as well as factors that have influenced our decision making. My son also can't swallow pills with the oral texture gag reflux challenge that he has with certain textures, so this caused it to be even harder for us when making medication choices as some meds can't be crushed or mixed with liquid to help.

At first, I was determined that Brian didn't need medication. I didn't want anything that would alter his personality or make him be "zoned out". To me, making a child "zombied" to make them behave is not helping with the behavior, it's only medicating them. To truly help, the right mix of meds must be found. I still feel this way but have found certain medicines to be beneficial when they don't have some of these ill side effects. The only problem is that to find the right medicine, it is usually a trial-and-error process. It's not easy, but I promise when you find what works, it is worth it.

Once Brian started to school, as he got a little older, we did discuss a few medication options with his doctor as a sweet teacher friend of mine, Mary, discussed things that could possibly help. I didn't want him on "mind altering medications." One profound statement that I will forever remember her saying to me is this: "Trisha, his mind is already a bit altered, why not check with the doctor to see if there is something that could help him think a bit more clearly?" Wow, I had never really thought about things that were happening in that light, but it was food for thought.

We then discussed medication options with Brian's doctor. I told the doctor that we wanted to try the less harsh medications with the least side effects. We found out about some non-stimulant medications which we tried first.

With little side effects, this worked well for a good while. We saw Brian focus more and it didn't "wear off" or have a "come down" effect as we had heard some of the other medications did.

As time progressed, Brian's doctor offered a new medical genetic test to see which other medications may better suit Brian's chemical make-up in our situation to see if any other meds could be more beneficial to help him. Unfortunately, this testing did not work for us. What was supposed to be the least harsh for Brian's system ended up being the complete opposite. It was a hard road of trial and error to say the least.

We found that Brian could not take certain stimulant medications that are a lot of times used to treat symptoms of hyperactivity associated with Autism and ADHD or ADD. Because of the success with other children, we tried different kinds of meds throughout the progression of time asked to do so; however, the side effects were much worse than the benefits. These meds completely changed his personality. I did not see a positive difference and even his teachers told us that this was not working as the opposite effects were much worse than just handling his challenges. I pulled him off as quickly as I could.

These were some very hard days for us. Brian would rage out of control with aggressive behavior which was not his normal personality at all and would also bite his hands out of anger and frustration. I hated hearing the negative comments from teachers because I knew that Brian was and could be a well-behaved child. He was very loving. He needed help, but this was not the answer.

I don't deny that some of Brian's tantrums were behaviors, (after all he is special needs), but very few of those were behaviors that couldn't be dealt with. A lot of his behavior, I'm sorry to say, had to be dealt with alot of times out of a misunderstanding that even well-meaning teachers or therapists didn't understand nor did some of them understand how to help Brian with his struggle of communication at times, or the many medication changes and side effects that we were experiencing. Until you have been there, it is not in your favor to make a judgment call.

Thankfully, through time and a lot of prayer for guidance and patience, we have found a mix of medication, school programs, and therapy programs that have helped Brian to thrive and strive to reach his potential. As we have continued this medication journey, we continue to use meds with the doctor's suggestions and help that have less side effects as well as continued sensory activities and therapy programs to help Brian.

There truly are some great meds out there to help children with varying disabilities to focus and help with mood regulation as well as "enhance" their personality and still be themselves. You don't have to destroy and diminish their personality to please others. Be a plugged-in parent and don't get talked into just anything. Take the time to research and talk with a Developmental Pediatrician or Psychologist who specialize in these disabilities and medication options and choices. There are great benefits to the right kinds of medications and therapy programs. You will know your child better than anyone ever will and though time and with God's help, as you work with the professionals as a team, you will find the best fit of both medication that works with your child's chemical make-up as well as therapy programs that work together to enhance your child's behavior and learning.

14

Epilepsy Found by Accident

ONE THING THAT we didn't know when we were trying medication trials was that Brian had Epilepsy. Because his seizures were silent seizures for many years, we had NO idea that he was having seizures of various types.

One of the medications that had been one of our trial medications had a warning label that said it was not to be used in someone with Epilepsy. We had NO idea that Brian had Epilepsy at the time. Unfortunately, when Brian was put on this medication it negatively enhanced his seizure activity and brought his seizures outward.

The very first time we ever thought of seizure activity, was when Brian passed out in my husband's arms in our kitchen. As he was going down, my husband caught him and then Brian started convulsing. That was one of the scariest times I will never ever forget. He convulsed for about twenty seconds then he started coming to. As he was waking up, he started crying. He was dazed, confused, and scared and so were we. We immediately called the doctor who advised us to watch Brian intently and call 911 if another episode occurred. We were also told that we needed to start charting and taping these episodes if they continued and if they became worse we were told to get him to the hospital.

However, even though this was horrible, it had a purpose because we had no idea that Brian was having silent seizures until it surfaced outwardly with convulsions after being put on this medication. We started videotaping what we called "dizzy episodes" at the time since Brian would appear "dizzy" like he was about to "drop" to the floor. We took Brian to his doctor and then he referred us to a neurologist. We were asked to keep video logs and chart of each episode.

Brian was set up for a twenty-four-hour sleep deprived EEG (Electroencephalogram) at first. This is a test that uses electrodes that are attached to your scalp which detects electrical activity in your brain. This test is used to diagnose and help monitor seizure disorders.

This test didn't really produce much of the results needed since Brian was sedated and asleep and not active or under stress or in situations that could trigger a seizure, although some seizures do occur when someone is sleeping. It was decided that he would be hospitalized and have a 36-hour EEG to have him monitored for circumstances that could possibly show the results as to what was happening. There are many varying triggers for seizure activity and although we anticipated that this is what was happening, we still had to find more answers.

Surprisingly, after admission into the hospital for this EEG test, the battery of testing didn't take all three days. Brian's brain impulses were showing the seizure activity by the end of the first day as well as into the second day. Brian's seizures were so strange. He sometimes would get "dizzy" and almost drop (also known as drop seizures or atonic seizures). His eyes would get a fixed glaze and he would just stare off (Absence seizures). He also showed signs of partial focal seizures that according to an accompanying MRI and brain scan were coming from the back and left sides of his brain. The MRI showed no brain damage but did show the impulse activity from the seizures on those sides of his brain.

Brian also had a few episodes of convulsions where his body would shake or where he would draw up on one side of his body and his mouth would draw up a bit at times, almost like stroke symptoms.

Here we were now facing an Epilepsy diagnosis. Epilepsy is a brain disorder in which seizures which produce brain misfires in certain nerve cells causing at times a semi- or total loss of consciousness. We had now found the need to educate ourselves with Brian's particular type of seizures to understand Epilepsy in addition to Autism.

Thankfully, we found two medications that worked well with Brian's chemical make-up and could be taken with his other medications. They not only helped to balance and control Brian's seizures, but they also helped with his autism and mood regulation, so in turn, they added a dual purpose.

Brian still struggles occasionally with his seizures. Although more controlled, at fourteen years old now, we must continue to monitor and chart his seizure activity along with medications dosages; however, we have seen huge improvements and for this we are grateful.

Brian also has now grown to understand at times when he seems to feel one coming on (almost like an aura) with certain triggers and he has learned to let us know by his body language. I'm thankful he understands now when something doesn't feel quite right. Although this has been hard, I am forever thankful that we found out this piece of Brian's puzzle that was missing that helped us to understand more of his struggles and how to help him.

15

Genetics

AS PARENTS, RICK and I wanted to continue to find out everything that we could to help Brian. Brian was almost ten years old before we explored Genetics. Looking back now, I should have known that this could be a contributing factor, but I never really thought about it until one day at work.

A teacher friend of mine, Angela, had a son with special needs and had explored this option with her family. They received some answers to their son's disability and she and I talked about possible options for our family. She was very helpful during this decision-making process, so much so, that Rick and I decided to talk to our doctor.

We decided after looking at our family trees and the histories of our families, to explore the Genetics division to see if we could find more answers to our incomplete puzzle. With bloodwork and testing for Brian in the genetics division of the healthcare system that we were already a part of, it was determined that Brian had a chromosome deletion disorder, 1Q21.1 Microdeletion Disorder which is a rare disorder that affects chromosome one. It was also thought that he may have a second chromosomal deletion disorder as well, but the criteria changed, and this chromosome deletion disorder was the only one actually confirmed and diagnosed.

Anyone ever have parent guilt? For years Rick and I blamed

ourselves, thinking somehow, we could have somehow accidentally contributed to Brian's delays. Rick, as a machinist, had always worked in certain types of chemicals for machine operation and so he blamed himself thinking maybe Brian's challenges could have somehow been his fault since he had to work with certain types of chemicals on his job to clean machine parts. I blamed myself because early in my pregnancy, I struggled with a sinus infection and took Sudafed, which had a warning label, "Do not take while pregnant" that I didn't see until after I had taken the medication. The doctors weren't concerned about it at all, but it still made me question if this was somehow partly my fault.

For ten solid years, Rick and I struggled with Brian's delays. The stress, the worry, and not knowing the whys was tough. We just wanted answers. It was a huge sigh of relief for both of us to learn about 1Q21.1 Microdeletion Chromosome Disorder This disorder also explained a lot of traits that Brian had. It was through these results from the genetics division that we realized that Brian was wired this way. Some of our genes may have contributed to how the chromosomes came together, but our son was perfect, a creation of God almighty, and we were so thankful to have some solid answers to our mounting questions.

Some families choose not to explore genetics because they don't want to know if genetics plays a part in a diagnosis, but we are so thankful that we found answers to our questions. Getting involved in genetics is one of the best decisions that we ever made and really gave us insight and more understanding as to what was happening to our sweet boy as the chromosome deletion disorder was linked to other traits and previous diagnosis'. We were also able to continue to research and learn all we could about any other options that may help us in our journey.

16

"Little Progress is Great Progress"

DID YOU KNOW that in today's time, the statistics show that one in forty-four children are diagnosed with Autism in the U.S.? Boys are more likely to be diagnosed than girls. Thirty-one percent of children with Autism Spectrum Disorder also have intellectual disability. Genetics can play a part with other underlying disorders. (autismspeaks.org).

It's scary to hear a "label." Hearing a diagnosis for your child can be heart wrenching, in fact, heart breaking. Once you can move past the initial shock of a diagnosis and overcome the "what ifs" you will learn to lay aside those fears and focus on the gift that you have been given. Autism is not a death sentence. In fact, it is a gift that God chose to give our family to teach us about life and unconditional love. We have learned so much about progress. Each child learns at their own pace. Brian has proven that with time and patience, he can learn and grow in his own strengths, and we are amazed at how much he has learned. To our family, "Little Progress is Great Progress." We have learned to celebrate each little accomplishment comparing it to a runner winning a marathon. As we keep running the race, we win every single time that we watch more miracles each day as new growth happens, and new things just seem to "click" and make sense to our sweet Brian as he navigates through this world.

Each day we wake up to the gift of our son, we are thankful. As we continue throughout his teenage years, we are finding that he is growing and maturing in ways unimaginable. We know in our hearts that although he may never be on age level or grade level with his typically aged peers, we strive every day to make Brian as successful as he can be and hope that he will be able to maybe one day have some sort of job skill and be able to function more independently. One thing we know for sure, the way he hugs us and makes eye contact with us tells us that we have done something right. Many things that were once not thought possible for Brian, has proven untrue and he has surpassed what many thought he may not understand or accomplish.

Brian has progressed so much and while others may not understand, or may think it's minimal, the data from the bar graphs and charts from where we started to where we are now show great progress. We praise God to be as far along as we are. Although more moderate in his disabilities, Brian has worked so hard to accomplish so much. Brian is potty- trained and likes to take a bath to be clean. He is learning the importance of hygiene. Brian can brush his teeth, put on his clothes and shoes, and help with some household chores.

We may have to help him with these things at certain times on occasion, but he understands so much more with each day that passes, and he can do things and understands more each day as we teach him. We are grateful to help him daily learn self-help skills along with chores just like any other child. We continue with some academics as well as his communication skills that will continue to help him thrive as he gets older.

We take nothing for granted. Every little progress made means so much to us. We celebrate every little victory, every new skill learned, and every new connection that is made.

Brian is socialized at community events as well as church activities. We make sure that he is around others that may have "differing abilities" as he does, as well as typically developing peers. We not only try to help Brian be aware of others that may not understand him; we also see the need to help others grasp Brian with his "differing abilities." We strive to also educate those around us with diversity and education of special needs to promote both inclusion and advocacy as well as unconditional love.

One of the most heartbreaking and painful whispers of my heart surfaces when I think about what will happen to Brian after Rick or I pass away or can no longer care for him if sickness comes, or some sort of tragedy happens. Where will he live? Will he have someone to help him and love him? Will he be okay and not mistreated?

Some days, I can't allow my mind to go there. In today's world, I would never want my baby, even as he grows into a man, to ever be mistreated. Rick said he will just live with us forever. My heart's cry is for Jesus to come back and to take us all to Heaven together.

It can be so heart wrenching as parents of a special needs child to think of group homes or assisted living homes. I'm sure there are great ones out there, but of course, it's so hard to think about it as there have been stories to surface where people have been mistreated or harmed. I hope that when this time comes that Brian will understand that we didn't just leave him or desert him. It is great to have service coordinators and professionals in place that can help aide when the time comes to make those decisions.

Thinking about the future and trying to have plans in place is a good thing to be preparing for which we are doing each day, but I also must remind myself that God will always have Brian in His Almighty Hands. I must remind myself that Brian belongs to God and belonged to Him before He sent him to both Rick and I to take care of.

How does our teenage years look for Brian? Right now, we choose to bask in the sweet young man that he is becoming. He may never have a girlfriend or drive a car, then again, who knows? He may never have the "dream job" or finish college. While teenage dreams look different for us, and it sometimes breaks my heart, we allow Brian to enjoy the things that he appreciates most in life on his level. Some of it may be way below his age range while some of it may be age appropriate. We watch as he is hitting puberty and maturing sometimes watching and hanging out with typical peers in a typical setting, yet other times standing out as "different" with his delays. We see the little smirks of maturity as he watches and notices pretty girls yet holds onto his Elmo movie and sings or hums his preschool songs at times.

Sometimes, it's not easy watching typical age peers of Brian and thinking of where we should be in relation to where we are. When my mindset shifts to this, I must remind myself to let that go and stop worrying about his " I can'ts" while continuing to focus on his "I cans." While these deficits surface from time to time, I couldn't love my son anymore than I do right now. I have learned to enjoy this sweet boy who God gave us. He is so genuine and loving. He loves to give us hugs and high fives and still craves our attention. He will need us forever. He may not fly his wings at eighteen years old like most children do, but I promise you he will fly. He will soar. He will reach his potential.

Each day he continues to make us proud. He has so many supports and his loving family that will be with him every step of the way. Brian has a purpose. God has reached so many people through the miracles and testimony of our sweet boy and God continues to do miraculous things in Brian's life every single day.

We have always spent a lot of quality family time with Brian and plan to continue to do so. We continue to go on vacations, plan and prepare fun activities that engage him that we all enjoy, and show him daily how much we love him. In a few years we will need to start preparing for what adulthood looks like for Brian. That is so hard for me to believe; however, I know that it is coming. As I watch him grow, I remind myself that he will continue to learn and progress at his level and on the time frame that God allows.

Today, we are better people because of our son Brian who has been our teacher. Rick and I have learned patience and unconditional love. We have empathy and understanding of others in situations such as ours. We have been able to reach out to other families through all that we have learned, and God has given us more understanding to reach special needs families through not only friendships but also through ministry.

So, where do we go from here?

We continue. We allow God to continue to teach us by performing even more miracles in our lives through this special gift He gave us, our very own special needs son, Brian.

17

My Dad, The Bionic Preacher

GROWING UP AS a preacher's daughter, I remember my mom (Sandy) and my dad (John, Sr). always telling me, my sister, and my brother, to always have faith in God. That seemed easy enough at first until there were tests that came. Tests that we were not ready to pass. Tests in life that made you question the whys and hows especially when you had no experience or qualifications to answer the questions and no way to study for the final exam. Sometimes you often wondered what would happen next in the journey of twists and turns that had to be traveled.

Being a preacher's kid (PK) was sometimes a blessing and sometimes a curse, but one that I personally would not trade for anything in the world. My siblings and I learned a great deal about faith in uncertain times, spiritual values, morality, unconditional love, and compassion.

I can't begin to tell you what my daddy and his call of God on my life has meant to me or the impact it has made on my life. I felt the tug of God on my heart at just seven years old. I'm so thankful to have been saved at such an early age after one of my dad's messages as the Holy Spirit worked in my heart. I've made some mistakes at times but I have always tried to serve God and God has always been faithful.

Every single time something happened unexpectantly, it was faith that always persevered over fear. Now don't get me wrong, there were plenty of times we were afraid and plenty of times where we wondered if God would come through. But not once did He fail us, ever, even if the situations and answers did not come in a way that we expected.

My dad was drafted into the army right after high school. He and my mom were married at a young age shortly before my dad was drafted. Being in the army, my dad went to Korea and served as a helicopter mechanic during his time of service. Daddy was honorably discharged and earned an apprenticeship as a machinist. Daddy also earned a Bachelor of Applied Science in Bible from Bethany Bible College.

My dad was a Bi-vocational Pastor, and in the early days of his ministry, he not only pastored, but he also worked a full-time job as a CNC machinist. Daddy was so busy yet took time with us as a family and his example of faith has radiated in my times of need on more than one occasion.

We would jokingly call my dad the "Bionic Preacher". With his bridle bone condition, even though it was a milder case of Osteogenesis Imperfecta, he still suffered several broken bones and had to learn how to use his limbs all over again on more than one occasion while having surgeries to put his limbs together with pins and rods.

One traumatic memory that I recall from my childhood is of an incident that happened to my dad when I was only five years old. My dad had been cutting grass at the church and around our church parsonage where we lived. At the time, the church parsonage had a screened-in back porch attached. Dad had made a makeshift ramp up the steps to drive the mower up the ramp and onto the porch.

I was playing on the swing set outside and as dad was driving up the ramp on the lawn mower it unexpectedly flipped over with my dad on it and the lawn mower landed on top of him as he was crushed underneath.

My mom was at a women's auxiliary meeting, and they had gone out to eat and at the time I had no siblings. It was just me and my daddy. I was young but I knew my daddy was hurt. I went running over to him and he was coherent, and his face and head were visible, but he was in a lot of pain. He said, "I need you to call 911 for an ambulance."

For a five-year-old, that was definitely a traumatic moment, but I'm so thankful I knew how to call out for an emergency. After a few minutes which of course seemed like an eternity, an ambulance arrived and helped my dad get onto a stretcher. As they helped him get out from under the lawn mower, I remember crying as I was extremely terrified, and I knew he was severely injured. My mom was contacted, and daddy was transported to the hospital by ambulance and my mom and I made our way to the hospital.

My dad had to have emergency surgery to put back together the crushed vertebrae in his back. He also had multiple bones that were broken. With therapy and time in a wheelchair as well as an extensive healing and therapy process, my dad learned how to walk again as he had to do numerous times before with his bridle bones. He has had multiple broken bones from various situations throughout his life, but God has always raised him up.

Although daddy struggled with multiple issues, he continued to pastor as well as work full time. I have never known such strength or such faith. There has never been a lazy bone in my dad's body, even though his bones were bridle with the diagnosis of Osteogenesis Imperfecta.

My dad has always inspired me in so many ways. He has always told my siblings and I not to worry and that God always has every situation under control. I have watched faith and strength lived out through my dad in unimaginable ways.

Daddy has always quoted scriptures from the Bible. My dad has always used a lot of scripture from the Bible in his messages and this has always helped me to memorize and hide God's word in my heart. It just came natural for us to memorize Bible verses because daddy has always had a scripture to share for life's situations.

There was one Sunday morning that I recall that will forever be etched in my memory. It was a typical Sunday morning. Sunday School had ended, and the worship service at our church had started. The choir had just finished singing and my dad got up as normal to deliver his sermon.

Although daddy was quoting scripture which were always parts of his sermon, he began to repeat himself repeatedly. He became confused and his face began to draw on one side. We knew then what was happening, he was having a stroke.

Reluctantly, we were having a tough time getting daddy to understand what was going on. He kept saying in a slurred voice, "I know something is happening to me, but I have to finish what God laid on my heart". Our church members were patient and on top of things. We got daddy help.

By the time we got to the hospital, daddy had experienced a series of mini strokes. Daddy did recover thankfully, although it has affected his short-term memory on occasion. What amazed me through it all though, is that his scripture memorization never went away! Thankfully, daddy had a great recovery and has continued to do well over the years continuing to work in ministry.

My dad also suffered with Bell's Palsy as well as some additional mini strokes in his eye that made his eyes cross for a small amount of time. I'm so thankful that he also recovered from these situations which were all very scary and unexpected. My dad refused to allow circumstances to damper his spirit or challenge his faith. He has always relied heavily on Proverbs 3:5-6: "Trust in the Lord with all your heart; lean not to your understanding, in all your ways acknowledge Him and He will direct your paths".

Another memory that I will forever hold close to my heart is the time that my daddy got sick close to the Thanksgiving holidays. My daddy had to be rushed to the hospital fighting Guillan' Barre' Syndrome which was severe and had to be treated with a series of strong antibiotics as well as Occupational and Physical Therapy.

His body had began to shut down and he became paralyzed from the infection. It was highly probable that the disorder was caused by taking a flu shot vaccination as my dad had a flu shot a few days prior. It was a very scary time and with the holidays approaching, we were terrified not knowing what to expect.

Prayer warriors everywhere began to pray for our family. As a few weeks went by, my dad started to get better. He was moved to a rehabilitation facility where he completed Occupational Therapy and Physical Therapy to strengthen his limbs as well as get them working again.

We went to visit my dad in the rehabilitation facility that he had been moved to after church on Sunday morning after the weekend of Thanksgiving that year as dad was not at home for the holiday. It was definitely a different Thanksgiving, and we were heartbroken to miss our family Thanksgiving meal.

I remember that my dad told us to be strong and have faith. As he was laying paralyzed in that rehab room and learning to use his limbs again, it's my daddy's strength and strong faith that I remember the most. He told us not to be afraid and to put our trust in God. He prayed with us, even from his bed in his rehabilitation room.

He never once denounced his faith. He knew that God would raise him up. He would not believe anything different, and he would not allow us to do so either. He claimed his healing by faith. He began singing the song, "I'll Be Home for Christmas" to me, my siblings, and my mama that day as we were leaving.

Daddy, in his own way, now had his heart cries reaching out to us through this very song. To this very day, I tear up every time I hear this song throughout the Christmas season.

In tears we hugged him and left while we prayed that his dream would come true. Not only was daddy home for Christmas that year, he also was moving in and out of his wheelchair again and learning to walk gain, just as so many times before with the brittleness of his bones as well as paralyzed limbs.

Dad had learned to walk again with a cane and limited mobility, but he was walking. He was hanging Christmas ornaments on our Christmas tree. We were all home and together for Christmas just as daddy had sung to us. I truly considered it a Christmas miracle, sort of like a Hallmark movie.

When Christmas day approached, I opened some presents that I had wanted, but I opened a gift from my daddy that meant more to me than any money could buy. It was a birdhouse. One that my daddy had worked on to strengthen his hands in rehab. One that I knew was made with a lot of love and pain all while he learned to use his hands again. A simple birdhouse that I will cherish forever.

With every Christmas holiday that passes, we are reminded of God's goodness. We never take for granted our time spent together as a family. God truly does perform miracles. Sometimes it just takes faith, even if it is just the faith of a tiny mustard seed, to believe.

I'm also reminded of God's provision through times of sickness and financial strain that occurred with work lost due to illness and surgery. We would pray. God would hear. Mom would open the mailbox, and someone would send a card with money. A refund would come at just the right time to pay another bill where medical expenses just happened to be overpaid. Churches that were affiliated with ours as well as our church took up money and sent it to our family. My daddy always worked hard but when this happened, it was heartbreaking at the time because he wasn't physically able to continue working. We saw God's hands move in ways of provision for our family that I will never ever forget. Daddy and mama had always given to the ministry financially as well as physically and sacrificially and had helped people at times with money or groceries or specific needs that no one knew anything about. I watched as they reached out and gave sacrificially and benevolently.

Even through all these hardships, not one bill went unpaid. I saw evidence of God's provision as it came back full circle when we got in situations like this. I watched God provide in ways unimaginable and just at the right times. Daddy has always said you can never outgive God or go wrong by helping someone. I've watched that prove true in so many circumstances.

He continued to pastor our church and even worked on his ma-chinist job from a wheelchair until he just couldn't work on a public job any longer. He then met the criteria for disability, although he was still able to do some odd and in jobs as well as continue to Pastor. Thankfully, he got his walking strength back and he was able to walk with a limp and a cane as he still does to this day.

Many times I think back to my dad's childhood where he shared with us how he lost his daddy at the age of 59 (my grandpa who I never got to meet on this side of Heaven), while his mom, my precious Grandma Moena, kept a house, worked, raised her family, and taught values that I know lives with my dad until this day. I am so very thankful for a mom's love that my grandma radiated to my dad and his siblings (all my aunts and uncles) that made them the adults that they are today.

I miss my Grandma Moe especially around Christmas time. She always had a beautiful Christmas tree at our Christmas gatherings at her house and we came together as a family, cousins, aunts, uncles, daughters, sons, and extended families. Those were always fun times at Grandma's that I will forever cherish.

My daddy is still with us and continues to shine the light of Jesus into others as he continues to preach and feed the hungry through a ministry called "Care and Share" at Victory Free Will Baptist Church.

A favorite verse that my dad has always reminded me of in challenging times is found in Romans 8:28 "And we know that all things work together for good for those that love God, to those who are the called according to His purpose."

Things may not be "good" as we go through situations that are painful, but they work together "for good." It may take time, healing, patience, perseverance, and prayer, but things truly do work together to benefit our journey with God.

A day does not go by to this day that my dad never fails to send a scripture to me daily by text or at times on social media as well as countless others that he encourages daily. His constant reminders of God's grace and goodness continue to make my heart smile daily. I am so thankful that God hand-picked my dad for me and I'm so thankful to still have him here with us.

Although my family and I now attend different churches, hearing my daddy preach never gets old. If you've ever heard that song, "Thank You for Giving to the Lord," by Ray Boltz then you know that I'm forever grateful that my dad is my earthly father and because of his obedience to God, I also have God as my Heavenly Father.

18

My Superhero Mom

IF I EVER knew of a superhero in my life, it is my mama. My mom is not only my best friend, but she is also the best mama in the whole world, hands down. She is a cancer survivor and a true-life warrior. Every time I hear the song "Wind Beneath My Wings", by Bette Midler, I think of her as this song reminds me so much of her and her strength and resilience. She has been my motivation and encouragement in life as well as one that pushes me to keep going when times get tough. It's humorous, but she has always said that when life gets tough, you got to put on those big girl panties and just deal with it.

My mom had a tougher childhood in some areas that really was never up for public display. During those tougher days of her childhood my mama sought her refuge near a grapevine. A grapevine that I am sure heard many conversations to God and watched her cry many tears while she poured out her heart cries to God. My precious Grandma Grace did the best she could do to love and teach my mom and her siblings and loved her children dearly. Mama recalls many good times even through the tough times, and Grandma Grace was one of the very best.

As I watch my mom, I am so thankful for my grandma Grace. I think about how much my mom favors my grandma in so many ways. Grandma Grace had a very fitting name, "Grace". I will always remember she had a heart full of kindness and smiles and offered food to eat upon every visit. She always had a clean and very tidy house and had such great hospitality, which are all traits that my mom portrays and has portrayed to others all her life. I miss my grandma but know that we will see her again in Heaven one day, along with my aunt Dorothy, (Toody as we called her), who also modeled "Grace" in her everday walk in this life.

I look up to my mama so much and have learned so much by watching her example. She reminds me so much of the Proverbs 31 Scripture from the Bible. She was always up before everyone else, making sure we all had food to eat, a clean and tidy house, and making sure that we had all we needed to start our days off on the right foot.

Mama seems to have had very many rare never ending unforeseen circumstances on and off throughout her journey in life. In addition to being a colon cancer survivor, mama has endured a great deal of difficulty and stress but always continues to put on a smile and push through.

Mama suffered the loss of three children during her pregnancies. She lost one before I was born, one before my sister, and one before my brother.

Technically, my siblings were also considered miracle babies. So often, my sweet mama tells the funny story of me as a child. I was fussy. I was dramatic. Can you believe it? Me? No, never in a million years could I imagine myself ever being this way. Bahahaha!

My mom and dad decided that I would be an only child, so my mom had a tubal ligation completed. About five years later, my mom and dad decided that they wanted to try again to have more children, so they talked to a specialist for mom to have surgery to reverse the tubal ligation. Winston Salem Baptist Hospital was up for the challenge. Mom had the surgery with only a small percentage of being able to conceive again.

When I was about eight years old, I was playing with two baby dolls that I absolutely loved. One doll I decided to name Lisa and the other Dianne. I was not sure why at the time, I just thought they were pretty names. Little did I know mom was going to announce to me that her and daddy had found out she was pregnant with a girl! I asked my mama if we could name my sister Lisa Diane after my baby dolls. To those of you who know my sister, you know that Lisa's name fit her perfectly. Insert heart emoji here.

Two years later, my mom also conceived again and became pregnant with a boy! My brother, John Jr., was born around Christmas time and was named after my dad as the only son. We joke with my mom a lot because my brother was born on Christmas Eve. We told mom she should have hung on longer to have my brother on Christmas Day, which in turn is my dad's birthday as well. As we all know, though, when a baby decides to come, there is no "holding out any longer". So, my mom brought home my brother for Christmas Day once discharged from the hospital.

Miracles didn't stop there. One day many years ago mama also developed a virus which caused her to lose her smell and taste for over a year. I've recently edited this paragraph because of the pandemic. It's crazy, but all these years later, we tell her that COVID 19 existed back then even though this was way before the year 2020.

Doctors had told my mom that her smell and taste may not come back so to be prepared to learn to function without it. We continued to hope and pray that she would be ok. It would take over a year, but God restored it!

I will never forget the Sunday morning that my mom got her smell and taste back the first time as we were getting ready for church and we were all working together to get out the door successfully, insert laughter here. It can get quite hectic in a preacher's house on a Sunday morning with a teenage daughter (me) and my younger siblings that needed help as they were young and only two years apart.

As we were all getting ready, my dad and mom were tag teaming it and my dad decided that he would cook breakfast that morning. He was cooking breakfast and in particular bacon. I never ever will forget as my mama came down the hallway tears streaming, saying "Johnny, I smell that bacon!" Daddy said, "Sandy, come taste it" With tears streaming, not only could my mama smell it, but she could also taste it! And then she tried the orange juice and the eggs. God had indeed brought back her smell and taste. Some say it was coincidence, but I say it was a miracle from God.

One memory that will forever remind me of my mom's faith and stamina was when she was diagnosed with colon cancer. She often felt sick in her early forties and knew something just was not quite right with her health. She began to lose some color in her skin tone and turned an ashy gray color. Through a battery of testing, it was found that she had cancer. Once finally found, it was detected that my mom had a tumor on her colon.

A cancer diagnosis is not something that you want to hear as a forty-three-year-old mama with a fifteen-year-old, a six-year-old and a four-year-old. Mama and daddy had talked about death. I know it sounds morbid, but when you are faced with the big "C" word, a lot must be thought about. Back when mom was diagnosed, although surgery and treatment options existed, the technological advancements in medicine that we see today had not occurred yet.

Mom talked to dad about making out funeral arrangements, just in case, not knowing the outcome of this situation. The unknown can really be scary, but though my mom's faith was tested, she continued to learn to trust in God. I know she questioned the whys. I know she did not understand at all what God was doing at the time. And her heart cries, I know, puddled the floor thinking of the possibility of death and leaving her family behind.

My Grandma Moe came to stay with us for a little bit during this time of my mom's sickness to help. She was there for comfort, love, and support. I will never forget how scared I was that I was going to lose my mama. Although I knew who God was and had felt his tug on my heart at seven years old and had given my heart to him, I had wavered from God and had doubted things as a teenager. I can remember my heart being broken into a million pieces. I promised God that I could help take care of my sister and brother. I was responsible for helping them get ready for school and drive them while mama had her surgery. I promised to help with their homework and help my grandma with the house chores.

I remember feeling so alone and helpless one night after helping my grandma get our bedtime routine completed with my sister and brother. My dad was with my mama at the hospital. I did not know at the time that my grandma Moe was close to my bedroom door, and I had no idea that she was watching and listening as I poured out my heart whispers to God.

Knowing in my heart, I needed to hear from God, I just didn't understand. As a fifteen-year-old heartbroken teenage girl, I felt scared, alone, and frustrated. I got down by my bedside. I was on my knees. I knew God, but I also knew my heart felt so away from Him at the time. I had wandered away from Him at times although I knew He was still there. I was just so heartbroken. I could not fathom how a God that could love us so much would decide to give my mama cancer. I hated the talk of death. I felt hopeless, helpless, and full of despair.

I had already previously watched how God worked amazing miracles in my family. I knew that God could heal. I knew that God was just. I knew that God was good. I had been told all these things all my life. In my heart, I knew it, but I questioned it in a big way during this time in my life and honestly, I wasn't so sure.

As I prayed by my bedside, I asked God why. I was angry. I cried those heart felt tears, you know the ones that come from that break in your heart that is so painful that you can't do anything but sob. Those whispers from my heart that only God could feel. Those sobs that felt like they washed out my whole heart on the floor.

In my prayer, I told God that if He could and if He would just reach down and heal my mama, I promised to serve Him with all my heart for the rest of my life. I promised to give Him my all. Some may have called it bargaining with God, but, honestly, I didn't really care what people thought. At this point in my life, I needed God to show me He was truly Who He said He was so that my faith could be restored.

I promised God that no matter what I would choose to love Him and that I would trust Him. However, I needed to have some assurance that He understood my heartbreak. And even if God did not heal her, I knew His Grace. I knew His Love, and I knew His mercy. I was not even sure at this point if He would even hear this heartbroken teenage girl, but between the sobs, I knew what faith was and I knew deep down I had to trust Him regardless of the outcome. I could choose to become bitter or better. That is a choice.

As the days passed in the hospital, my mama who herself was questioning in her heart why this was happening was reminded of God's Amazing Grace through a music box that a young couple from our church brought to her on a visit to the hospital. She did not know what music it played until she opened that beautiful music box in that hospital room after they left from their visit. The music box chimed out "Amazing Grace" one of my mom's favorite songs:

"Amazing Grace, how sweet the sound, that saved a wretch like me! I once was lost, but now I'm found, was blind but now I see."

What an awesome reminder to my mama as she was facing the unknown. She has reminded us over the years that the sweetest consolation came when she listened to it again and remembered this particular stanza of the song that she holds dear to her heart:

"Through many dangers, toils, and snares, I have already come! "Tis grace that's brought me safe thus far and grace will lead me home".

She was not sure if it would be her earthly home of which she longed for it to be or her Heavenly home of which she was ready to go. One thing is for sure, although she wanted to see Jesus, she did not want to leave her family or her kids.

Cancer Surgery Day for my mom came and went. The doctors were hopeful. From what they could tell, they had retrieved all of the tumor and cancer from the site. After mom's cancer surgery and recovery, she came back to her earthly home. I could never have imagined growing up without my mama and I'm so thankful that God heard the heart cries and whispers of this fifteen-year-old girl who wasn't ready to say goodbye.

That little music box was then passed on to a teacher that I had from school, (who was also a friend of mine's mom), when she was struggling with some health conditions. Mama wanted to pass the blessing along to help encourage someone else during a time of despair. Today we call it "paying it forward".

The only request that my mama had was for the music box to be passed along to the next struggling person that needed it once the teacher found someone else who may be struggling and may need some encouragement to help in their journey.

I often wonder where that little music box has gone all these years later and how many have been reached and encouraged with that little music box. I'm praying and hopeful that we can find that music box after all these years and learn how it has helped encourage others that may have needed hope.

A strengthening and comforting Bible verse that helped during that time was found in Psalm 103:1-5." I remember seeing these verses highlighted and bookmarked in my mom's Bible.

Psalm 103:1-5

Verse 1 -"Bless the Lord, Oh my soul, and all that is within me, bless His holy name. "

Verse 2- "Bless the Lord, Oh my soul, and forget not all His benefits."

Verse 3- "Who forgives all your iniquities; **who heals all your diseases.**"

Verse 4- "Who redeems your life from destruction, who crowns you with lovingkindness and tender mercies."

Verse 5- "Who satisfies your mouth with good things; **so that your youth is renewed like the eagles.**"

"Look at that again!"
"Who heals all your diseases,"
"So that your youth is renewed like the eagles."

I often wondered why my mom loves eagles so much. In my heart I know that this Scripture carried her through her cancer, just as an eagle soars above the clouds of their troubles and find strength.

God knew that mama would be a future nana to four beautiful grandkids. One of which would be my sweet special needs son who would love his nana so very much. The bond that my mom and my son Brian share has been so very special. Brian loves his Nana. He gives her hugs. He gives her high fives. He smiles. He makes conversations with her on his speech iPad. He tells her he loves her with not only his words from his speech device but also with his actions every time that we get to spend time with her. She has been a constant in Brian's life from day one. Every time we get to go see her or when we visit, he smiles.

After mom's surgery, she continued to not only hold the job of being a Pastor's wife, but also helped maintain the church with janitorial duties as well as help many who were sick. We jokingly called her the "taxi" driver as she would help our elderly in our church get back and forth to doctor's appointments and grocery store visits or just lend a hand when needed driving her own van or the church van. I remember tons of those trips.

My mom was always known as an encourager and one of her generosities was to give out flowers to others when she knew of a struggle or that someone just needed encouragement in their daily walk. She passed out many flowers to others. She has always had the saying, "Give them their flowers while they are living to show them you care." Constantly mom gave words of encouragement and hugs with flowers along the way.

As I write these words about my mom, I am so very thankful that God has allowed many more years to spend with my mom. As we now live every day to the fullest, we are so grateful even to this day to still have mom here with us until God calls her home.

Mom's wisdom and advice continue to help me on a daily basis. She is truly my best friend. Her support and encouragement help sustain me on hard days. And believe me, in our situation, there have been days that I didn't think I could put one foot in front of the other. But in my heart cries, there would be my mom cheering me on and not allowing me to ever think about defeat.

In her seventies now, she struggles with diabetes and osteoporosis as well as crippling arthritis, bone spurs, and most recently a knee replacement and toe joint replacement surgery, but it hasn't stopped her. She says that it is truly God's hands that heal her daily and give her strength.

Above all, when I think of a mother's love, I think of my mom. A mother's love is the closest to God's love that a person can ever find. Since mom has always told me to give flowers to those you love while they are still living, that would be difficult for me to do for my mama. I would need a whole garden! My mom is the best mom and nana in the world. If I could search the whole world over again, I'd choose my mom. Thank you, God, for a mother's love that is truly the closest to your love that I have ever experienced.

19

My Sister Lisa, "Tiny Dancer"

MY SISTER, LISA, was the middle child. She's been most recently tagged the name, "tiny dancer." Lisa has smiled and danced to the beat of music her whole life, but at times in ways some would never be able to imagine. Lisa inherited the bridle bone condition "osteogenesis imperfecta" from our dad. Thankfully, it was a milder case than some but one that would impact us all just the same.

As a little baby and child Lisa had a history of bridle and broken bones in particular her legs. Mom had to teach her how to walk multiple times. Lisa had a tiny frame and had casts from 3 months old and up and at one time was wheeled in a wheelchair until she could learn to walk again.

I will never forget her first broken bone. And it was my fault! Insert sobbing emoji here! In all seriousness, my mom was allowing me to hold her and help with her, of course with adult supervision. I loved her so much. She was like my real-life baby doll. She was three months old. Mom was helping me to lay her down and I didn't realize that her leg was bent under her. Normally that wouldn't have been a problem, but it popped her bone. You could literally here her bone break. Then a hurdling scream. I will NEVER forget that scream. I felt so awful!

We had no idea at the time that she had inherited Osteogenesis Imperfecta. That was only one little cast out of the series of casts that she would have. It broke my heart.

She had to have school at home until second grade but eventually got strong enough to be able to attend school.

Lisa grew and gained strength and stamina although tiny and had to be careful with activities that she did. She became a part of the little league cheerleading squad at Blessed Hope Christian School the school that we were privileged to attend and loved to cheer. She also loved music and loved to dance. Her legs that were frail continued to dance to the beat of music that radiated from her heart even through fragility.

Lisa also found her strength in helping others. She was able to tutor other children that struggled, one being a special needs student that needed help. Little did she realize that years later she would have a special needs nephew in my son Brian as well as be a nana to a special needs baby, little Neveah.

Lisa graduated from High School at Blessed Hope and went on to obtain her degree in Early Childhood to become a teacher. Helping others was her passion so it was no surprise at all that she wanted to reach out and use her God-given talent to love children and help them reach their potential.

As the years have passed, Lisa's bones have gotten stronger and even though she still struggles from her condition on occasion, she has learned to balance her life and situations with a positive outlook. Unless you knew she suffered from the condition, you would never be able to tell by the way she lives her life.

Lisa's personality has always been one of "determination" and "spunk". She has learned to laugh from joy in her spirit even when happiness was not there. Happiness is based on circumstances, but deep-rooted joy comes from deep within. Lisa learned that her situations in life did not define her, and she chose to face them head on dancing to each beat even if it came from many different drums.

Lisa married a wonderful husband and became a part of a blended family with girls and grandkids that she continues to love as her own. Blended families can be beautiful when God is the center of the relationship. God blessed her broken road and sent her the family that she longed for since she could not have biological children of her own.

Lisa and her husband Johnnie attend Catawba Heights Baptist Church a wonderful church family who also have a Christian Motorcycle Ministry called "Traveling Light". This ministry is known for their encouragement of others through rides of prayer, toy runs, and fellowship in rides to pray, uplift, and encourage one another.

July of 2017 was a year for my sister that tested not only her health but shook her faith. On a Traveling Light bike ride to Asheville, it began to rain. Johnnie and Lisa were going around a mountain curve on their motorcycle and the bike began to hydroplane. Johnnie did all he could to keep the bike up but it went down.

Thankfully, Johnnie's injuries were minor, although painful, with an injured ankle and foot. My sister, however, landed on the road, face down, with the bike on top of her. As she waited with her face on that asphalt for 45 minutes until the ambulance arrived, she was conscious and alert, but her body was in horrible pain and shock.

Her helmet was a mess and so was her body. Thankfully, she didn't have any head trauma but did sustain multiple broken bones. Her left side injuries included a broken shoulder as well as broken ribs, and crushed tibia fibula bones in her leg which required surgery. With her already weakened bones from the Osteogenesis Imperfecta we knew it would be quite a recovery process.

Lisa not only had surgery but also had to have an external fixation device until her bones in her leg could heal enough to have physical and occupational therapy. Her broken shoulder and ribs also took a while to heal.

Once again, she was learning to walk but this time as an adult. She wondered if she would ever get her dancing feet back and we all hoped that each day we would see progress. She was very transparent in her recovery, seeing both times of defeat and times of victory.

It was, however, in those moments of defeat that Lisa reached down to the depths of her soul and was reminded of the scriptures and faith that had sustained our family through so many other challenging times that would help her to see her hope and faith again even though at the time it was hard to grasp that God was holding her up.

Her heart cries poured out in tears puddling on the floor wondering where God was and what He was doing. She couldn't understand the why's nor did she realize at the time that God would use this tragic accident to perform a miracle and use her story for God's glory. I remember her tears of pain puddling around her as we would help her around her house do things that she once could do independently.

Lisa worked so hard to walk and gain her stamina to see her through to healing. Once again, with our family's faith being tested, with the tears that flowed and the questions that came, it was faith, faith that manifested itself in the God of Heaven who could heal. Faith that would sustain.

Although it was a lot of hard work, some months down the road, Lisa did get her walking feet back. In addition, she got her dancing feet back. Dancing was even a part of her therapy. It's no surprise, not only did music help sustain and encourage her, it was the comfort that God gave to help heal her not only emotionally and spiritually, but physically.

Not knowing then about my husband's cancer journey during this time of grief in Lisa's life, It would be Lisa who would offer help and hope when we needed it the most this past year. Through Lisa's very own testimony of faith, recovery, and healing from this motorcycle accident, along with her friends of faith with the Travelin' Light Ministry, we were blessed with an unexpected "Rolling Prayer" encouragement ride and a fundraiser for Rick as we faced medical bills from Rick's cancer appointments and chemotherapy. Isn't it just like God to take a tragic situation and turn it into a blessing for someone else?

Lisa's husband, Johnnie, has been a constant and an encourager. God blessed their broken roads and put them together. He knew the spouse that she needed, and their love story is an amazing one. God truly knows who we need to complete us.

Lisa continues to inspire me and so many others to dance to the beat and rhythm of life that God has placed in our lives. She continues to encourage and her love for her family and friends as well as of teaching children is a blessing to all who know her. I'm so very thankful for a sister that is not only my biological sibling, but one of my very best friends that I couldn't imagine doing life without. And I still take credit for her beautiful name.... Lisa.

20

The Christmas Baby Boy, My Brother

MY BROTHER, JOHN, was born as a healthy Christmas baby boy. He arrived on Christmas Eve and was put in a Christmas stocking to bring home. We always teased my mom that she should have held out her labor for just a few more hours so that my brother could have been born on Christmas day because that is my dad's birthday as well.

My mom and dad were told that there could possibly be some medical challenges with John because of my mom and dad's age. They even offered mom a test to see if she wanted to have an abortion. They had no idea who they were talking to! Of course, my mom and dad were not going to have an abortion as a pro-life preacher's family!

My brother, by the way, was born and he was just fine. Imagine the number of people who are given abortion as a choice when there should be other options given. How many lives are wasted because a child is considered a burden instead of a blessing? And being a mom of a special needs son myself, who we've watched learn and grow, I'm so thankful to be pro-life.

It was in High School that my brother decided to see a United

States Marine recruiter. He decided to join the marines and officially went in right after he graduated from high school.

Boot camp at Parris Island seemed to last forever. We wrote letters back and forth as a family to maintain contact and sent care packages with not only supplies and money but memories from home. At boot camp graduation I remember my parents being so eager to see my brother. John had done well in his training to graduate as a United States Marine. This memory now seems like forever ago.

As a Marine, my brother soon got called overseas. If you have never experienced a moment like this, it can be heart wrenching for a family facing the unknown. While so thankful for those who follow the call to protect our country, the realization of not being sure of the outcome of varying factors can be a huge worry to their family.

I remember many nights of my mom and dad interceding in prayer for my brother. Many nights of worry and tears from my mama's heart as she struggled with the unknown yet knew God could take care of my brother overseas. I know deep down my brother had to feel those prayers in those difficult times. My dad always tried to be an encourager and reminded my brother to have faith and pray.

My mom stayed awake many nights praying for my brother's safety and relied heavily upon Psalm 91 during those days. If you have never had the privilege of reading this scripture from the Bible, it is comforting and provides a prayer of protection. My mom not only relied on the entire passage of Psalm 91 heavily during those days, but also wrote It in words to my brother as a source of encouragement and strength for him to keep going even when times were difficult. Sometimes, even in our best efforts, circumstances and disagreements can separate a family in various ways. It's in these times that we place every situation into God's hands.

Although sixteen verses in length, I want to share Psalm 91 with you. It's a passage that I know God gave to us as a promise for comfort during those harder days. My brother, John, did make it home safely from overseas. He now has an amazingly awesome son as well as two beautiful daughters. Again, it's faith and the Faith Giver whose promises we relied on daily that we know brought him home and even in separation or disagreement, this chapter still holds true.

I hope this encourages your heart as it continues to be an encouragement to us each day. I'll end this chapter with this.

Psalm 91:

Verse 1- He that dwells in the secret place of the most High will abide under the shadow of the Almighty.

Verse 2: I will say of the Lord, He is my refuge and my fortress: my God in Him will I trust.

Verse 3: Surely, He will deliver you from the snare of the fowler, and from the noisome pestilence.

Verse 4: He will cover you with his feathers, and under his wings you can trust. His truth will be your shield and buckler.

Verse 5: You don't need to be afraid for the terror that flies by night, nor for the arrow that flies by day.

Verse 6: Nor for the pestilence that walks in darkness, or the destruction that wastes at noon day.

Verse 7: A thousand shall fall at thy side; and ten thousand at thy right hand, but it will not come nigh to you.

Verse 8: Only with your eyes will you behold and see the reward of the wicked.

Verse 9: Because you have made the Lord, which is your refuge, even the most high, your habitation.

Verse 10: There will no evil befall you, neither any plague come nigh to your dwelling.

Verse 11: For He will give His angels charge over you, to keep you in all your ways.

Verse 12: They will bear you up in their hands, so that you don't dash your foot against a stone.

Verse 13: You shall tread upon the lion and adder; the young lion and the dragon you will trample under feet.

Verse 14: Because He hath set His love upon me, therefore I will deliver him. I will set him on high because he has known my name.

Verse 15: He shall call upon me, and I will answer him: I will be with him in trouble; I will deliver him and honor him.

Verse 16: With long life will I satisfy him and show him my salvation.

21

Rick's family: In laws or Outlaws?

RICK'S FAMILY HAS always been considered my second family. I have never once considered them as outlaws, not even as in laws, but as family members. A family that I grew to know and love when I met my husband all those years ago before we got married.

Rick's childhood was a bit different than mine. He grew up with two older sisters (Lissa and Lona) and his mom. Rick's dad and mom separated when Rick was only a year old, so he grew up in his early years with a house full of women, bless him!

Rick jokingly talks about his sisters and how they always got away with things that he got blamed for. Truth be told, I always wondered if he being the only boy was not the spoiled one but he still blames it all on his sisters as he claims he was innocent. I just let them "duke" it out among themselves when they see each other. Insert laughter here.

Rick often talks of his childhood with a lot of great memories. For the most part, Rick and his siblings had a childhood full of love. However, he also has some very unpleasant memories from time to time which causes him to block out some of his childhood memories. I'm thankful that Rick and I can share everything including our heartbreaks in life, no matter what. There have been times that his heart has cried out with tears puddling on the floor as his heart whispers have turned to sobs.

Rick's mom, (Margaret, or Nana Mac as the grandkids called her), was very loving and caring. She worked hard to take care of Rick and his siblings. Rick learned to work hard and have a compassionate heart from his mom. She had so many precious traits that Rick has shown and continues to show in his daily life. She created such a loving home atmosphere. Being a single parent was tough, but Rick's mom did all she could do to make everything work together.

Rick's dad (Richard) and his mom (Margaret) had a bit of a shaky marriage early on. Rick's dad, although he had been raised to know about God, chose a different path in life. After Rick was born his parents decided that it was in the best interest of the family to go their separate ways.

During this time of separation, Rick's mom always worked hard to maintain her job as well as support her family. Rick watched his mama struggle to make ends meet but she never complained. Working hard was imbedded in him at an early age. Margaret succeeded in being "the best mom ever" as Rick says. She always had arms full of love and hugs to share and a smile to give. Her laughter and her smile were contagious.

Rick's grandparents who lived next door, were also a vital part of Rick growing up. Grandma and Grandpa Rowland always had food for everyone and a smile and hug to give as well. Rick's grandpa himself loved to joke around and his grandma was always full of stories to share. You never left their house hungry or without a trinket to take home most days.

Rick grew up as a typical boy who loved go karts and bike riding with his cousins who also lived nearby. His cousins, Richie, Davy, and Johnny were more like brothers to him than cousins as well as Brandy who was more like a sister.

One memory that is hard for the family even to this day and that will forever be etched into our minds was a traumatic moment of a car accident that killed Rick's cousin. At just nineteen years old, Richie, of whom Rick loved more as a brother than his cousin, was killed in a tragic car accident just miles from our home which shook our family to the core. It was heartbreaking. We had just spent some time with him the night before this happened and would never have expected this to be the last time that we got to spend with him.

To this day, Rick misses his cousin and talks about him. The funeral was held at the church we attended at the time with my dad officiating. One thing I will never forget is the number of teenagers that filled the church. Richie had reached a lot of people with his contagious smile and caring heart.

Although we know he made Heaven his home, it was still a shock and heartbreak to us all. Even in the sorrow, we know the hope of heaven and that we will see him again. It is just such a sombering thought to think that one day you are with a loved one and the next day they are gone. Life is so uncertain and times like this are a reminder that eternity is just a breath away.

As Rick entered his pre-teen years, his oldest sister Lona with his mom's approval, went in search of their dad. Richard (Rick's dad) had been living close to his family members in a different state and Lona found him and made the initial contact. God performed a miracle of restoration. Rick was around eleven years old when God restored his family. His dad and mom's marriage became reconciled, and their family unit was restored although it didn't come without a lot of hard work and dedication.

Rick was not only able to meet and spend time with his dad, he also was blessed to meet his other set of grandparents, aunts, uncles, and cousins as well as extended family members as God brought them all back together in a huge way. The connections and memories made from that point on have been priceless and we will always love Rick's extended family.

I'm so thankful for the restoration of Rick's family and the restoration of Rick and his dad's relationship. Rick blamed himself for his parents' separation for years because he was the baby of the family when his daddy left, and Rick felt like it was somehow his fault. Of course, that wasn't true but to know that on a firsthand basis helped Rick resolve this and gave him closure in his own heart. Rick's dad had also restored his relationship with God and became a minister sharing his testimony for a short period of time.

God can take broken things and put them back together. Are you broken? Do you need restoration? It can happen. Rick's family is a testament to this. It may take some time for healing. It will take a lot of commitment and dedication and a renewed and determined mind. But with work and God's help, broken relationships can indeed be restored.

22

Rick's Parents -Marriage Vows proved Through Sickness and In Health

WHEN GOD BROUGHT Rick's parents back together, the years ahead would really prove that vows could be restored and renewed even with health and unexpected sickness.

Rick's dad had inherited Huntington's disease, a neurological progressive disease which results in progressive movement as well as cognitive and psychiatric symptoms, of which we didn't' know at the time. It is genetic on his dad's side of the family (his grandmother had it as well as some extended family members), but that it affected his dad came to our family as somewhat of a surprise. My husband, Rick, was genetically tested at Duke University Hospital to find that thankfully he did not inherit the disease.

It was in our early married years that Rick's dad, Richard, began to show symptoms. We noticed small signs of the illness here and there which prompted a visit to the neurologist in which he received the diagnosis.

Richard, Rick's dad, fought Huntington's disease with all that he had for over 20 years and eventually became disabled. He was able to work on his job and function and enjoy life normally for a good while. The involuntary movements were one of the first symptoms noticed. As the disease progressed with each stage of the disease, Richard also developed problems with coordination, difficulty at times thinking and understanding, compulsive behavior and mood swings, hallucination, and paranoia all progressive symptoms that usually accompany the diagnosis.

Rick's mom, Margaret, was such a strong woman and stood by Richard throughout the progression of this disease. It still amazes us that God would take the broken marriage and home life that once tore these two apart and put them back together to love and help each other through these times of struggles and sickness.

Rick's mom was like a second mom to me. I never once thought of her as "the dreaded mother-in-law". In everything she did she brought such joy into the lives of everyone who knew her. She was a wonderful Nana (Nana Mac as we called her) to not only our special needs son but to every one of her grands and great grands.

Unfortunately, Margaret also developed some health issues herself during the progression of Richard's illness. Margaret maintained her job and continued to help take care of Rick's dad until her health began to decline to a point to where she had to slow down and leave her job to be able to continue to help with Richard's illness as well as try to continue to take care of herself.

As a diabetic, Rick's mom continued to maintain her sugar levels with insulin and diet. She unfortunately developed further complications along the way which landed her in the hospital in a diabetic coma and eventually caused heart problems. Margaret progressively got worse and had her first heart attack of which thankfully she recovered. A year later, her heart became very weak, and she developed congestive heart failure.

Over a short period of time, she began to further decline and became weaker as the days progressed. Rick's mom was given Lasix to help keep the fluid off, but it seemed it would always return. She tried to continue to visit and enjoy her life and we enjoyed hanging out with her as well as Rick's dad as much as we were able.

It was on Mother's Day of 2014 that we had been to visit Rick's mom and enjoyed a nice Mother's Day dinner. Rick, my son Brian, and I were very much enjoying this time with her and Richard. Brian acknowledged his Nana Mac on his speech device and said, "Nana Mac, I love you". It was his first time telling her that with his speech iPad device even though he told her a lot with his love and hugs. We were all in tears. Little did we realize this would be the last time Brian would get to see her.

As we enjoyed the afternoon with Nana Mac, we noticed that her legs and feet were swelling more than normal. They continued to swell throughout the evening, and she ended up at the hospital.

The next few days seemed like a blur. Nana Mac remained in the hospital. She was alert and talking. I was able to go and stay on Tuesday night of that week with her in between the times Rick's sister could stay. With Brian, my special needs son, my work schedule, and my husband's work schedule we were trying to make it work so that we could all visit with her as we were able.

Rick's mom and I enjoyed some serious conversations that night but also a lot of memories and laughs. We talked about so many things, and I never ever will forget the love that I felt for her as I watched her and conversed with her as she lay in that hospital bed. We watched Dr. Charles Stanley on TV and listened to an amazing sermon. He was one of Nana Mac's favorite TV preachers.

That night is one that I will never take for granted. I never knew that this very night would be the last time that I would see and talk with her on this side of Heaven.

As Wednesday morning came, I went home early so that I could get Brian and get him ready for school as well as head to work myself before my husband went to work. Around 11:00 I got a phone call at the school where I work. It was Rick's sister, Lona. She was telling me that Nana Mac had started to decline. Immediately a call was placed to my husband Rick.

Rick called his mom to talk to her and told her he loved her as she was alert at that time and told her he was excited to see her. Rick was getting off work to head to the hospital when the hospital decided that hospice would take over since there was nothing more to be done there. Rick's sister, Lona, called Rick and his sister Lissa to let them know that Nana Mac would be coming home, and they wanted Rick to go to their house to open the door for them and get things ready to make her transition home.

23

Eternity in View— Passing from this Life

I'M LITERALLY IN tears as I write this. Rick's mama had fought long and hard. Her body was tired. Her spirit was preparing for departure at this very moment, but we didn't know it. Margaret was going home, but not in the way we expected. She passed from this life to her Heavenly home before hospice could even get her ready to be transported. With tears and heartbreak, Rick's sister Lona called Rick to let him know that she would not be meeting him at their house.

I received a call from my husband shortly thereafter. His voice was cracking, he was trying to fight back the tears. He told me that his mom had been carried by the angels into Heaven. Oh, how he longed to see her. He had been preparing for her arrival at her house. He had made her a nice comfortable spot moving furniture around to get into a hospital bed. Rick was ready to see and talk with his mom. With sobs, he said "Honey, I never even got to physically say goodbye." Although he did get to talk to her on the phone and tell her he loved her, he was wanting to hug her, help her, and hold her hand. This is hard on Rick until this very day. He knows he was doing what he needed to do, but Mother's Day that year was the last day he got to kiss her on the head, hug her, and see her.

With numbness and sadness, we proceeded with the funeral arrangements and the memorial service. It was surreal to say the least. It was also during this time that Rick's dad was rapidly progressing with Huntington's disease. It was a lot to take in and accept all at once. Rick and both of his sisters continued to grieve the loss of their mom all while trying to remain strong and help care for their dad.

Rick and Lona would switch nights in between work schedules to go and spend the night to help with any needs during the nighttime as well as check on him in between the health care workers during daytime hours. Rick's sister Lissa who lives out of state continued to be supportive both emotionally and physically as much as possible. They continued to be a loving family as well as supportive throughout all the heartbreak with the loss of Rick's mom as well as the progression of Rick's dad's illness.

One of the most painful and hardest memories that I have of Rick's dad during the progression of the disease was when he was in so much pain that he would lash out at others which wasn't his typical personality.

One night as Rick was trying to help his dad, Richard was in so much pain that he just wanted to die and expressed that to Rick aggressively going after him in a tussle. We all know it was the effects of the disease but to this day this heart wrenching moment is such a tough memory for Rick as he had to remain calm to get his dad calmed down, but the progression of violent behavior was getting worse. It was heartbreaking not being able to help someone you love in this mental capacity that was declining.

Richard started to lash out at some other family members as well as the grandkids. The family had some very difficult decisions to make. Because of the progression of the disease and the care that was going to be needed, Rick's sister and his siblings discussed 24-hour care.

Rick's sister Lona, being the primary caretaker, consulted with Rick and his sister, Lissa, to discuss next steps. A care facility that specialized in Huntington's disease was on the priority list. Not every place accepts patients with this disease because of the severity of the symptoms so it was quite a challenge for Lona to find a close placement.

Finally, a care facility was open to accept him. The only problem was that the facility was over three and a half hours from his home. It was heartbreaking to say the least, but we knew he had to be placed in a facility that could handle his needs. It was with a great deal of heartbreak, but this was the best decision for the family that had to be finalized.

Rick and his sisters made the trip to the facility as much as they could to help facilitate any needs he had. It was very difficult with Richard being so far away, but they did the best that they could in the unexpected situation that we had.

It was about a year after being placed in the facility that Richard developed a horrific kidney infection and it landed him with sepsis. A PICC line was inserted to help with medications, treat infection, and manage his quality of life for as long as possible.

We were so very thankful for Rick's aunt, Cherie, (Richard's sister), during this time as she also travelled to the facility to help as she was able to assist and encourage the family. She and Rick's grandfather Campbell as well as his other extended family members were such a tremendous help through all of this because having had the heart-break of watching their mom (Rick's grandmother) go through the progression with Huntington's disease, they knew about the disease and how heartbreaking it was to watch the downward spiral of the progression.

Thankfully, after the PICC line was inserted to help with Richard's quality of life, Richard had a miraculous recovery because they had not given much hope. The quality time that was spent with Richard after this incident was time that we will never ever take for granted.

About five months later, in October, Richard lost his fight with Huntington's disease. Although the loss was difficult, his suffering had ended. We knew Jesus welcomed Richard with open arms, and oh, what a reunion in Heaven as he and Margaret (Rick's mom) were re-united along with all the family members that had gone on before.

Recently, over the past few years, Rick has had two of his dear cousins pass away as well as his grandfather Campbell. This has been hard on his extended family. We know the hope of Heaven and that we all will be reunited one day. The eternal home in Heaven with Jesus sure beats the suffering of this life; although it still leaves a huge gap in this life as we miss our loved ones so very much.

Holidays are always a bit hard for Rick. He misses his mom and his dad as well as his other family members and so do I. Brian even at times looks under his family folder on his speech iPad at their picture. I know he remembers. Oftentimes, I catch Rick listening to old voice messages left by both his mom and his dad to just hear their voices. Rick was closest to his mom although he and his dad had built a great relationship. The loss sometimes seems unbearable and even though healing does come throughout the process of grieving, it is never the same and the loss is always a broken missing piece of our hearts.

Even in the times of our suffering there is hope. I can't end this chapter with sadness. The years that go by give us hope. Hope of seeing our loved ones again in heaven. Hope that Jesus offers us with salvation. Hope that we pray others see in us to help them keep going, even in suffering and loss.

A scripture that gives us consolation during these moments is found in Revelation 21:4 - "And God shall wipe away all tears from their eyes; and there shall be no more death, neither sorrow, nor crying, neither shall there be any more pain; for the former things are passed away."

We have that hope. The hope of heaven. Hope of seeing our loved ones and being together with Jesus for eternity. A hope that we pray you can find no matter what you may be facing in life at this very moment.

As we move on to the next chapter, I cannot leave this one without telling you of the hope and love found in Jesus Christ especially as eternity is very real in passing from this life to the next. The love of Jesus runs deep, so deep that He gave his life for you on the cross to pay the penalty for your sins. The bible tells us that all have sinned and fallen short of God's glory. But the hope in this is that if we confess our sins, He is faithful and just to forgive us and remove our sins as far as the east is from the west with the promise of Heaven for eternity.

Prayer scares a lot of people, but honestly it is just talking to God, just as if you and I were talking. Pouring out your heart to Him. Telling Him that you want to be a Christian and make Heaven your home. Your problems will not all disappear, but the comfort and hope that Christ can give will make them easier to bear.

If you need guidance with prayer, you can pray a short simple prayer like this:

Dear God,

I confess my sins to you. I know that you loved me so much that you sent your son to die for me in my place and that He conquered death. I know that within myself I cannot obtain salvation. I believe in faith that you love me and will forgive me and that you can help me to deal with my current life circumstances as hard as they may be. I want to ask you to come into my life and guide me. Please give me comfort and strength to face my circumstances and guide and direct my steps.

In Jesus' name I pray.

Amen

24

"Growing up"

MY CHILDHOOD WAS amazing and worth every minute. I am so thankful to have grown up as I did. Some say I was too sheltered, but I didn't care. I always thought as a little girl that I wanted to be a missionary. Little did I realize that my mission field would one day be raising a special needs child and helping encourage other families that have special needs children or loved ones by sharing our story.

My parents and my family were considered a remarkably close -knit family. My mom and dad did the best they could to provide a loving and stable environment and spend time with us even in all the chaotic moments of jobs, church, and school.

I learned how to ride a bike as well as drive a car in the church parking lot since we lived in the church parsonage. I remember setting up trash cans and learning to parallel parking between them. Well, at least for the driver's test. Insert laughter here. You would never believe how many trash cans I hit in that parking lot trying to park. Parallel parking and well at times parking in general still present quite a challenge for me! Just ask anyone who has watched me park a car!

I have great memories of our family time together. We were so very busy as a preacher's family but still had time to eat our evening dinners together and enjoy time with both of our parents even through such busy times.

I will never forget each night that my daddy would call us together at 9:00 pm before bed- time when he was working as a machinist on third shift in addition to pastoring. We would have a devotion and have prayer each night before he would have to leave again.

Looking back on my childhood, I honestly don't know how my parents did it nor how they held it all together. As daddy continued to work full time and pastor, we continued to have Sunday morning, Sunday night, and Wednesday night church services as well as Gospel Singings, Fundraisers, youth activities, senior activities, and revivals. That was the day when churches had five full nights of revival. It was busy, very busy to say the least. Mama maintained our house, along with helping me and my siblings in all our difficulties and filled in the gaps where dad needed. She made sure we were fed, bathed, helped maintain homework and school activities as well as tried to find some-time in between to relax herself.

There would be times when daddy would work all night, but a member would be scheduled for a surgery in the hospital, so he would clean up and head on to the hospital to help encourage and pray with the family as well as sit at the hospital until they didn't need him any-more. Then he would come home and sleep a few hours and go at it again. It amazes me now as I look back and wonder how in the world my parents made it all work.

We seldom missed a vacation except the times that my dad and mom were sick. Family time, although limited at times, meant so much to us and my daddy and mama always made sure to make our child-hood memorable. They sacrificed a lot to make sure that we always had fun times together even as busy as they were.

They sacrificed to send us to a Christian school to obtain a Christian education and supported our sports activities and cheerleading activi-ties and allowed us to have fun in what we could excel in. They made it to our ballgames, made sure we made practice, and encouraged us with both wins and losses.

I never will forget all of our trips to Gatlinburg and Pigeon Forge Tennessee, Beach trips, our once in a lifetime Disney world and Sea

World trip, Carowinds, Ghost Town, Santa's Land, Go Kart track fun, Kings Mountain Battleground cook outs, etc., in between all the craziness! I honestly don't know how my parents made the world go 'round' but all I have are great memories-awesome memories that I will never ever take for granted.

I think, to this very day, this is the very reason that my husband and I have sacrificed so much to take our special needs son out and about in the community as well as make sure he learns how to have fun and enjoy vacations as well as parks, stores, and restaurants. I pray he always holds these memories in his heart. I want him to remember how we had fun with him and enjoyed life with a heart full of joy.

Growing up in the parsonage also warranted those fun special times of helping around the church. I remember my siblings and I helping to clean and vacuum the church with my family as well as straighten hymnals and offering folders and making sure each bench and each row had what was needed for service. We helped to change the sign each Sunday. My childhood was truly blessed, even in the craziness of our life.

To be very real with you, we did indeed have our share of "growing pains". Preacher's families are real people just like everyone else. I had some moments in my childhood and teens that I am not proud of. I remember having to ask for forgiveness more than once. Being a "Preacher's family" did not mean that we were perfect, in the least. We just tried to maintain the best we knew how.

I had my share of disciplinary action from my parents from time to time as a child and into my teen years even though I was conscientious and tried not to create a lot of problems because I really wanted to be a good child and did not want to disappoint my parents. In my pre-teen and early teen years, I also wavered some in my faith. I made some mistakes that disappointed my parents because of peer pressure and wanting to "fit it." I had to learn some life lessons but I'm so thankful to have had my parents to help me through it all.

Being put on a pedestal and having to have such a transparent life was not ideal. At times, things were not ok. We just did the best we could, apologized when we messed up, and trusted God for the rest.

I have a lot of good memories. You know, like the in the Movie, "Inside Out," where Joy is constantly reminding the other emotions to remember the good times. I remember the wonderful environment at Blessed Hope Baptist School. The teachers were amazing, and my siblings and I had tons of fun times growing up there.

My junior high years presented quite a few challenges. It was such a hard age and peer pressure was tough. I made a few decisions during that time that I'm not proud of. I'm so thankful that it didn't take long for me to decide that I didn't really want to be in with the "popular" crowd and the life lessons that were learned.

In high school, I loved being on the volleyball and basketball teams and riding "Old Big Red" our Blessed Hope School Bus to ballgames. Those were such fun times. Singing and cheering on the bus. Celebrating both victory and defeat of the wins and losses of ballgames. Interacting with team-mates and friends. Stopping to get something to eat afterwards and being crazy teenagers hanging out. We all loved our "Flames" Letterman jackets. At the time we thought we were pretty cool! And above all, we had so much fun. I will never forget those times. I am so thankful to have experienced them at our school.

Preacher Wayne Smith's vision of having a Christian school at Blessed Hope is one that I will forever be grateful for. Preacher and Mrs. Smith were role models to many of our students there. Preacher Smith always had a kind word, and his smile was contagious. His brother-in-law "Paw Paw" Cook, and his wife Mrs. Cook, were everyone's adopted grandparents. I give a lot of credit to Mrs. Grant (Mrs. Murphy), who was the best English teacher ever. She instilled in my soul a love for writing as her love for English made me strive to write out better essays and write out my thoughts in detail. The love that radiated from these adults will forever be held in my heart as well as the teachers and staff that made our school one of the very best.

Becoming a successful adult, I am so thankful to have had the opportunity of a Christian education at Blessed Hope. I am so thankful that God allowed my paths to cross with everyone there and I'm so thankful to have made life-long friendships of which are still intact until this day.

25

Meeting "The One"

THE FIRST TIME I met Rick he was with his family, and they had visited our church with his older married sister, Lona, who had previously visited and invited them.

While we all know what it's like to have that "butterflies in your stomach feeling," it truly happened to me when this tall, dark, and handsome young guy walked into our church around Valentine's Day, where my dad pastored.

He walked in. He was cute. He had pretty eyes. He had the most amazing dimples I had ever seen when he smiled. I thought, man, it would be so nice to know who this guy is. Befriend him. Find out more about him.

So, you would know, I set my mom up as the preacher's wife to make the welcoming introduction. Just kidding! In all actuality, my mom always welcomed new families to our church, but this time she had a few extra questions.

She approached him saying "hello" young man. Welcome to our church. I just wanted to find out your name and how old you are and let you know that we have a lot of great teenagers here. You are welcome anytime.

This heart-struck teenage girl really wanted to get to know this guy better. It was such a great idea that my mom wanted him to get involved with the teens. I am so glad she decided to "befriend" this amazing guy who she did not know at the time would become her son-in-law.

As the weeks went on, I got my nerve up to go over and talk to Rick and introduce myself. Yes, I know what you are thinking. Typical Preacher's Daughter. In all honesty, it really wasn't like that at all. At the time, he thought I wouldn't be interested, and I was feeling the same way but thought hey, if I can just work up my nerve to introduce myself and talk to him maybe he will want to be friends. I walked over to say hello and we talked for just a little bit that Sunday.

The next Sunday, I decided to ask to sit with him and his family. He told me "Yes, that would be great." Shortly after this, we decided to exchange phone numbers. Rick asked for my number first. It didn't take long, and he called me! I was so excited when my parents answered the phone and said, It's Rick! I was ecstatic to say the least. The next few months my heart fluttered with heart-struck joy every day as I woke up.

As we began to talk more about things that we enjoyed, were interested in, and were "officially going together" within a few months of talking, even though he technically had not officially asked me, I was already considered his girlfriend. I was fifteen at the time and I wasn't officially old enough to date until the "official" dating age of sweet sixteen per my parents.

I was able, however, to go on youth group outings with Rick with our church youth group. We also had fun at the Blessed Hope ballgames and enjoyed being together. Rick went to a public high school in the next city over from where we lived.

Because we lived in the church parsonage right beside of our church, Rick also was able to "walk me home after church and youth group outings". Mom and dad began to invite him over for Sunday dinner. Then I was able to go home with his family for Sunday dinner as well. We got to spend time together even though not officially going on a date until we both turned sweet sixteen.

I will never ever forget one night as Rick walked me home from church. And well, I got a goodnight kiss. Right as my dad was walking to the door of the house. He said, "Hey boy, whatcha' doing to my daughter?" Probably scared Rick to death! But it's all good. Rick decided to stick around. That was thirty-one years ago now!

I'm so thankful that God seen ahead of time that I needed Rick in my life at fifteen years old. It was during this time in my life that my mom was diagnosed with colon cancer. God knew I would need a shoulder and a best friend. Little did we know it would lead to five years of dating and then marriage all those years ago.

Sweet sixteen finally came. We were finally able to go on our first "official" date, alone. We went out to eat steak. I remember being shy and bringing most of my steak home. Ya'll, it's ok to eat with your man. I have learned over the years, there is no reason to go hungry, bahahaha! I can't believe I starved that night.

A lot of great drives and laughter ensued as we "cruised" during these dating years, and yes with the loud music and thumping speakers. We had plenty of mall dates, skating rink dates, out to eat dates, ballgame dates and just a lot of fun among ourselves that we would not trade for anything in the world.

Rick and I chose to stay away from the "party scene". Rick's family was separated because of this lifestyle. He didn't want anything to do with the party life. Rick knew the effects of alcohol and how it affected families.

My parents had taught me that alcohol can cause you to lose control and do things that you wouldn't otherwise do if you were sober. It could cause car accidents, overdoses, and addiction. My parents had great advice and I understood that more as I got older. I'm thankful that they took this stand in our house.

They also knew that as a preacher's family, choosing to abstain from alcohol was an overall moral decision. I never remember a time when alcohol was allowed or even in our house. My parents had made a commitment to choose a higher standard. A lot of people tell us that we were "sheltered" or so that is what everyone had said. But looking back, I'm thankful that my parents had these standards.

Honestly, I personally chose not to drink alcohol because I really didn't want to. It was my opinion that if I didn't drink, I would never have to worry about getting drunk. The Bible didn't necessarily say "Thou shalt not drink", but there were enough warning scriptures in the Bible that warn against drunkenness to make me stay away. Some people feel that they can handle the alcohol. Self -control is important and I just don't want to put myself in a situation like that just in case.

Alcohol has been used for ailments and medicinal purposes. Some have argued that Jesus drank with sinners and have talked about the miracle where Jesus turned water into wine. My personal conviction was that the wine that Jesus had was not used to get people drunk. After researching and studying the topic, the wine that was used in Biblical times may have had a very little alcohol content if any at all for preservation, but it was watered down and Jesus Himself warned against drunkenness. There are many differing opinions from many theologians and many Christians on this issue. When approached with the question of "Should a Christian drink alcohol?", I give my opinion and convictions as well as scripture that help me to abstain. Every Christian will have to make their own choice on this topic. Some feel as I do. Others feel differently. I personally abstain for my own convictions from God's Word.

Although Rick and I chose and still choose to make this decision we try not to make that judgement call for others. We both have friends and family members who have other convictions and some who also choose to continue to abstain as we do. I tell people that they need to base their convictions on standards based on God's Word.

I guess other people, especially some of our friends, thought we were also weird because of our convictions on sexual purity. As a young couple, Rick and I chose to be abstinent from a sexual relationship until marriage. We wanted to get to know each other but just not so intimately at such a young age. We wanted to learn and enjoy each other's personalities and have fun together without the physical attachment involved with premarital sex. We wanted to create a friendship and not just a relationship.

It was during this time that Rick and I decided to take a "True Love Waits" pledge at a youth conference that we attended with our church youth group where sexual intimacy and purity until marriage were promoted. It was because of our Christian walk that he and I decided to honor God together in our relationship and make that commitment not only to each other but to God.

Knowing my boundaries, I truly felt that sexual intimacy was sacred and something to be shared between two people within the boundaries of marriage. My parents always had always tried to promote saving such intimacy for a marriage relationship with commitment.

Rick was so respectful. He truly wanted to be with me and not for what I could offer or give physically, but what I could offer as a person and as a friend. I was amazed at how he genuinely enjoyed interacting with me. Having fun and laughing at our silliness yet sharing a love that could only be seen in our eyes. Hands to hold and hearts to bond but in so many more ways than I could have imagined.

Also, we knew that an unwed teen pregnancy could occur, and we knew we were not ready at that point to bring a child into the world. We were still growing up ourselves! Rick and I decided sexual purity until marriage is what God wanted from us and we wanted to honor Him above everything else even with the peer pressure all around us. God also knew our future journey of raising a child with special needs.

As time went on in our dating years, it became harder to fight the temptation. Just because we chose to wait for sex until marriage did not mean that we were not normal or that we did not have the desire to be with one another intimately. We just chose to continue to have the mindset to keep that commitment that we both promised to each other and to God until marriage and tried to avoid circumstances that would make us break that commitment even at times riding around with a Bible in the car on our dates. Now don't get me wrong, we enjoyed dating immensely. We just decided to save the best for last, a decision of which we are forever grateful.

During this time we became mentors as well as youth leaders for our youth group at our church at just eighteen years old and helped with our teens leading our youth to understand the importance of having Jesus in relationships. We listened to their struggles and wanted to help them and knew that we needed to be an example of faith. We wanted to be good role models to them and wanted to make sure that we were leading in the right direction.

The decision that we made to save sex for marriage is one that Rick, or I will never ever regret. Even now after twenty-five years of marriage, we still enjoy those cherished intimate moments and honestly our honeymoon has never ended. We truly have fun in more ways than we could have ever imagined, even in our intimate moments which are shared in private.

26

Proposal and Marriage

AS TIME PROGRESSED, Rick and I just knew it was God's plan for us to eventually get married. We knew if we could laugh together, tell each other anything, cry on each other's shoulders, pray together, and love each other as well as wait on each other to share our most intimate moments together, that we could surely build a life together. We were already best friends.

Rick proposed when we were both eighteen years old. I remember that he had a wooden box that was in the shape of a heart. He got down on one knee as the traditional proposal goes and gifted me the ring. To some it may not seem like an extravagant proposal, but it was the most special and cherished day in my life!

My sweet teenage boyfriend had worked long and hard after school on his job at an auto parts store to buy me a diamond. It wasn't the biggest diamond according to what some would consider "bling" and some may even scoff. But it's what I wanted. I have worn it since I was eighteen years old. And now, even after 25 years of marriage, I still tell people, you can have your fancy, I'll take the simple. Because it's been tried, tested, and true. He also received my parents blessing that night.

We finished high school and began college. We then got married two years after this proposal and started our new life together.

We graduated college in our early married years and had so much fun enjoying one another. Excited as a newly married couple, we also learned what it was like "adulting". Working and paying bills, learning how to be responsible, and figuring out married life was something that we realized would take time, patience, and experience.

Just like any other couple, married life has been both so exciting and frustrating all at the same time. From those very intimate moments to the hardships and the tears and the laughter, we have realized over time that there will be times when we have it all together, yet times when we would be very broken, falling apart and needy. I am so very thankful we learned how to grow closer together as we tried to figure out the ins and outs of our marriage through it all.

Realizing our marriage would be far from perfect, we learned that disagreements would ensue and that we would have to learn how to forgive and kiss and make up. Truly we learned what it meant "to love and to cherish" and "to have and to hold from this day forward."

It was during these times that God was preparing us for our life with Brian, our special needs son, even though we did not realize it at the time. We learned how we both responded to arguments, both good and bad. We learned how to be gentle and compassionate with each other's needs. We wanted to be sensitive to each other's feelings all while compromising when necessary to come to agreements when needed.

We learned about holding on to each other "through sickness and in health." Especially with the sickness of our family members and all that we had been through together and would go through a little later in our marriage, that we didn't even know about yet, including a child with special needs and Rick's cancer.

We had our share of financial struggles as well, understanding the concept of "for richer or poorer", through the trial and error of mistakes made as well as job losses, debts owed, and money management.

Our vows were and still are sacred. We still take them very seriously. We seem to grow deeper in love with every day that passes, even working through various struggles that would have torn most couples apart. It is amazing what can happen in a relationship when God is at the foundation.

We have always remembered and continue to remember some advice that my daddy gave us in our marriage counseling. Marriage is a love triangle, but not in the way that you may think. When my daddy did our marriage counseling, he gave us some profound wisdom that has continued to help us in our marriage until this very day.

We all know a triangle has three sides with three points. If you look at a triangle you will see two bottom points and one point at the top. The two bottom points are spread apart. On the bottom point on the left is the husband. The right bottom point belongs to the wife. The top point of the triangle belongs to God.

If the husband starts to move toward the top on his side, and the wife on her side, you will notice that the closer they both move toward the top point who is God, the closer they both draw to God and each other.

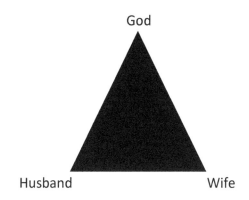

The opposite, though, has always been true as well. If the husband or wife are not as close to the pointing foundation (God) as they need to be, it has proven true that the marriage relationship isn't as strong and will suffer.

This advice has been and will continue to be a constant in our marriage. It has proven true time after time. We grow closer in our relationship together as we draw closer to God. If one or the other one of us has wavered, it has caused problems and difficulties that we had to learn to work through to reset our focus.

Although we have had our difficulties just like any other married couple, through it all, we have forgiven. We have loved. We have held each other tight when we wanted to give up. We have kept our focus on love, not on selfishness. We have made sure to keep our eyes fixed on each other, being faithful and true to one another, even when we could have been unfaithful. We have decided to continue to honor and cherish each other and continue to love each other even when it was hard.

Marriage can, at times, be challenging, but it can also be the biggest blessing ever. When given commitment and dedication, marriage can be the best friendship and companionship that a person can ever experience in this life with your soulmate.

27

"Will it ever end?"

WE HAVE SEEN many hardships throughout various circumstances and although we have seen God's very Hands at work as He brought us through so many difficulties, there were once again tests that we were given that at times were extremely hard to pass. Exams that tested our faith and made us question why in a very authentic way, but tests that we would learn the answers to in time. Answers that would give us hope throughout our situations even when we didn't see it at the time.

A few summers ago, Rick, Brian, and I had gone to a fun little go-kart park in our area called Adventure Landing for what we thought would be a fun family filled day. We had been so many times before and Brian loved it. Brian was so excited as we waited in line for the go-karts. He ended up usually riding with Rick in a two-seater and I had a one-seater. We were having a great time. Brian and I also loved the bumper boats.... Well until the day I almost drowned! Yes, drowning can happen in only three feet of water.

Brian and I had waited in the long line, and we headed toward the bumper boats. Unfortunately, I chose to try to get on first and then get Brian on before the attendant made it over as they were very busy, and Brian was having a hard time waiting. So, I put my foot on the boat to try to get on and get Brian on and then it happened. The boat shifted and I fell in the pool submerged as Brian fell on top of me. I didn't know at the time that Brian was on top of me, as things feel so differently underwater, and I couldn't' see nor get out. I was terrified and tried to find the wall. I was also hurt as I heard my leg pop as I twisted and went under. In my head, all I could think was that Brian was also trapped and drowning, "I have to get to my baby," I thought. "Oh, God, help me!" Rick was still in line on the outside of the fencing, and I was terrified not knowing if Brian was underwater too with his special needs.

After what seemed like an eternity, Rick saw Brian and I were in danger and jumped the fence as he and the attendant came running over. As I was pulled from the water almost going into a semi-conscious state of passing out, Rick assured me that thankfully Brian was okay and not injured. Brian and I were both soaking wet and as I tried to get up off the concrete I couldn't stand up and felt severe pain. I wish I would have gone on to the doctor that day, but I didn't. Brian was crying, wet, and ready to go. I limped to the car in pain but Brian and I were both alive and safe.

Into the night and the next day, my leg stayed pretty swollen, and the pain didn't stop so much so that I ended up at urgent care where I was told it was sprained. The x-ray didn't show a fracture and that it would heal in time. However, over the next few weeks, I continued to have pain even though we resumed life as normal with school and work activities.

In all actuality, I had two meniscus tears and a torn ACL in my leg that would be found some time later that would require surgery. The meniscus tears were fixed with a minor surgery, but the ACL remains torn to this day. The ACL surgery would have been more extensive, and I knew with Brian's special needs I could not be down for that long period of recovery, so I opted to strengthen my other muscles around the ACL with Physical Therapy. Thankfully we have both recovered and are fine.

Fast forward to 2019 and into the year 2020, and here we were fighting a pandemic in the United States as COVID 19 hits. Rick and I both end up having COVID, but thankfully we were okay, and Brian was too.

It was in his early twenties that Rick completed his degree and got a job as a machinist where he had worked for over twenty-three years. Rick thought he would remain on the job that he was at forever.

Until……

Rick's business suffered as the economic hardships of COVID 19 hit, and his job was affected. He was furloughed. Once again, we are thinking, wow, what else? How are we ever going to ever make ends meet? Especially now as the economy is tanking.

It wasn't long and then, God heard our prayers once again as Rick found another job within a few weeks of his layoff and God continues to provide for our family through this job with my husband's hard work and expertise as he has always been the bread winner in our family. It's ironic though, as his current company is literally right next door to his old place of employment, he is bringing home more money, his shift differential works with my son's school and therapy schedule as well as my work schedule and the company is graciously working with us as we maneuver through this cancer journey.

Finally, things were again starting to make sense even though we didn't see it at the time. As we look at our current circumstance, Rick is so much happier in this new job with less stress even though it's in a different field of employment. Isn't it crazy how God can take what looks so bad, and make the situation better than one could ever imagine, all in His timing? Little did we realize when he started this new job a couple of years ago now, that we would be facing a cancer diagnosis which would require better insurance and even more of a flexible schedule, but God knew that ahead of time didn't He? His provision was perfect even through a job loss.

28

"God's Got This!"

BACK TO REALITY now, here we were back in the year 2021 on the day of this cancer diagnosis, and I finally have made it home from my job interview. Rick and I hug and hold onto each other for just a few minutes as we both are still trying to process the news. Rick knew he had to go on to work that evening, so he got ready to head into work on second shift. I spend some sweet time with Brian playing some games and watching some videos. That night after Brian went to sleep, I laid down thinking about Rick and hoping that he was okay. The reality had not settled past the "numbness" and "shock" of our news, and I knew Rick would put on a brave face and do what he had to do at work and make it through his shift without telling a soul.

I cried myself to sleep knowing Rick's shift would be over in the middle of the night and he would be home. Maybe we could sit down together while Brian was sleeping and really take in our news and our next steps.

Rick works on twelve-hour shifts and usually has weekends off. It was Thursday night, and I was so glad to hear Rick's truck pull in our driveway in the stillness of the night. As he walked in the door, again, I wanted to hold him, love him, caress him, stroke his hair, and just let everything release as my whispers of my heart drowned his shoulder in hot wet tears.

He and I talked about a lot of things that night. I was scared. I wasn't sure about any of this, and I still didn't understand why God would allow this situation, especially here and now. I knew Rick was trying to be strong and deal with his news at his own pace, so I tried to allow him to do that. It just seemed that he was holding everything inside, I thought that I was the one with all the emotions that I couldn't seem to control.

It was early Friday after midnight as we continued to talk for a bit, but I knew Rick was tired and he needed to go to bed, so Rick laid down to sleep after his shift before getting Brian up to go the middle school. I was getting ready for work and as I got to work that day, I didn't say a word to anyone. Holding this news in was the hardest thing in the world as I wanted to just melt away into an ocean of tears, but I couldn't tell anyone yet. Rick wanted us to wait a bit to process our news before sharing which I completely understood. Our family members would all know soon, but we had decided to wait a few weeks before announcing our news to everyone else.

My sweet mama knew Rick and I needed some alone time that weekend. Brian is worth every second and we love him so much. He is never a burden, but being special needs parents, at times, you just need a date, together, alone. Mama volunteered to keep Brian for us while we went out to eat on a date at Longhorn. We ordered our steak, ate what we could in between talking and processing our news, then rode over to a local park where we could just enjoy some time to sit for a bit and walk and talk on a scenic trail.

Before we got out of the truck, we had the radio again tuned to 106.9 The Light. At a peak moment of silence in our conversation, both of us looking out of his truck window, a new song that we recently had grown to love "Help is on the Way" by Toby Mac, who is another one of our favorite Christian artists, started playing.

As the song started, I watched Rick's face as he had tears puddling in his eyes. I watched as this strong yet gentle man of mine released his "whispers of his heart" right there with me by his side. As the song played, the song melted him as I watched the release of his emotions.

He and I sat with no words between us and only the "whispers of our heart" flowing in tears down our cheeks as the song began. Rick grabbed my hand and while holding my hand on one side he raised his other hand to heaven as in the stillness of that moment, as if to say, "God, I let it go, and God's response to Rick's spirit in that very moment was "It's okay, I got this." Rick has adopted that motto and that has been his response throughout this whole journey. We may not understand, but we know, "God's got it." With tears still streaming, we both started singing along.

After the song went off, Rick and I held onto each other for a bit. He kissed me as our tears intermingled together as well as our lips. He expressed all that he was feeling, but even, in his deepest thoughts, he told me," Trish, I know we are going to be okay. God's got this, I know He does."

Moving forward with the diagnosis, we would find out the next few months about his treatment plan and would endure months of chemotherapy and radiation as well as continued treatments that would eventually cause Rick's immunity to bottom out to the point that he would have to be out of work for a few months, but as his cancer actually went into remission, he was able to go back to work a month earlier than expected. We were so excited to finally hear some good news and get a good report.

Thanksgiving dinner with our family was so awesome as we processed this bit of good news. We then decided to take a small mini vacation of remission celebration to our favorite vacationing spot in Gatlinburg, Pigeon Forge, and Sevierville Tennessee. My husband loves the Apple Barn and The Apple Valley Farmhouse Restaurant. They have the best apple fritters with Apple Butter. Rick was so excited to get his "fritters," as he finally had normal taste buds again since the chemotherapy had ended and the metallic taste from the chemo was gone. His smile that day made my heart leap into infinity as I thought about all he had been through, and this was "his moment" and "his celebration."

Christmas was awesome and we had so much joy as we really

understood the gift of the blessing of life and each other. Material things meant so little. Life is a vapor. It's short and it's important to focus on that quality time that is spent with each other. These moments together were more important to us than any earthly treasure. Brian had a great Christmas. We all did. It was time to ring in the new year.

So... 2022.... Watch Out
Here we come!

29

"Stronger" – But how?

AS WE RING in the New Year of January 2022, we were so happy to finally be back into our "abnormal normal.". We were just getting past the previous eleven months and breathing a sigh of relief and then....

"BOOM! There it hits," "Out of nowhere!"

As the doctor calls, we hear the news that no one wants to hear. After a routine PET Scan follow up, the doctor says, "Mr. Campbell, your cancer has returned in two new areas." Rick was just as shocked as I was as he was feeling great, no weakness, no fatigue and no signs or symptoms.

As Rick and I both sit together again to process this news and we both are in shock and disbelief, and although we both were extremely disappointed, again, Rick tells the doctor, "I'm going to be fine. God's got this."

Once again, here we were, in all the questioning, more afraid because of such a quick relapse, yet this time, instead of anger and blame, we find that we are both thanking and praising God for what

He is about to do. I can't tell you that we were both like, "Yay! It's back!" Rick said, "Man I was hoping for good news," and although he knew God would be with us, this was harder news to process as he had been in remission. He and I both looked at each other and then at Brian who was with us and thought again about our next steps.

Understanding that God is a God of miracles, Rick looked at me and said, "Trish, I don't understand this, but God has a plan. He has a purpose for this, and we will be okay."

As we shared our disappointing news, we had so many tell us, "Wow, you guys are so strong." Your faith will carry you." "God hasn't brought you this far to stop now." Rick and I appreciated all the comments, but I thought, man, I sure hope we can get through all of this.

This time, the treatment plan was referred to another doctor in the same practice but one with more extensive knowledge of relapse and how to treat. We would find out that Rick would undergo more chemo and once his cancer was in remission, we would be getting prepared for stem cell extraction of his own cells as well as a stem cell transplant with additional chemo. We wanted to go for the highest possible chance of treatment and survival, yet we knew that God was the Ultimate Healer, and it was ultimately all in His Hands.

This time, once again, as Rick goes into work, I am still trying to process our news of relapse. A bit scared yet knowing God's Hands were holding us up, I decided that Brian and I would take a drive. Brian loves to ride and listen to music just like Rick and I do. We are a music family. There is just something about belting out tunes in the car that our family finds comforting.

One of my favorite Mandisa CD's that I had purchased a couple of years earlier was the selection for the drive. Mandisa has been a vessel that God has used to speak to my heart so many times. Her testimony through her own journey of depression that was triggered by losing a friend of hers to cancer has been instrumental in picking up my spirit on some dark days. Her transparency of sharing her story from her "Out of the Dark" story and songs that came from this time in her life has picked me up out of my own depression pit more than once.

I didn't want to admit that I had been in a "funk" of my own, a depression state if you will, but I realized when listening to her testimony on You Tube one day that some days I was just going through the motions each day, taking care of my son, working, and being a wife, smiling on the outside, yet, my inner spirit felt so broken some days and I just wasn't sure if I could do this again. I didn't want to be disappointed again. I didn't want Rick to be sick again. I wanted it all to be fixed.

As Brian and I started the car, my sweet boy was excited that I put in Mandisa. He loves to dance to her songs by rocking back and forth in the back seat and so I selected one of our favorites, "Stronger." As Brian "bebopped" in the back seat, not really understanding the magnitude of all that was taking place, I sang and listened to that song like I never had before, holding back my tears....

Sometimes I do wonder if things will ever get better. Staying up all night and sleeping in between the heartbreak of my tears, at times, I have found myself so desperate to be reminded of the old saying that says, "No pain, no gain." When I thought about that not only in a physical sense, but also in a spiritual sense, I was reminded that to get stronger, endurance must be built up by weight. The weights aren't easy and as you strengthen your body, your muscles become sore, yet the strength and stamina gained when the weights are lifted help your body to get fit and remain healthy.

In relation, the weights of this world sometimes seem so overbearing and make our spiritual muscles ache. It's in those times that you remember how your past circumstances have built stamina and endurance as you overcame the struggle. I was reminded of this strength in this song as I knew that God would take these situations, lift the weights, and give strength and stamina to endure our next steps.

The bridge of this song is taken from the Scripture found in Philippians 1:6 which says," Being confident of this very thing, that He who has begun a good work in You, will complete it until the day of Jesus Christ."

My heart immediately went to those "whispers" as Brian was

dancing with his sweet smile in the back seat as the song played on repeat over and over for the next thirty minutes as we drove.

As I watched him in my rearview mirror, I thought, "Okay God." You started a work with Brian. Rick and I are not the same people we were before you gave us this special child to love and guide. You gave us Brian to teach us about your unconditional love and patience. You are not finished yet. I need my husband. Brian needs his daddy. Most of all, we all need to be restored.

This time, God, I am looking at this cancer not in blame and defeat, but in testimony and praise. I don't understand, but I choose to praise. No matter the outcome, you have proven that we will be okay.

I said, "God, Rick is a fighter. You didn't bring us this far to stop our story. You started this work in our lives and you will be faithful to complete it, if only we will believe it." My heart then finds release again as I knew that God had spoken through Mandisa's song and that scripture of reassurance. You will complete our story for your glory, if only we believe.

30

"Stand in Faith" to the End

SO, HERE WE are. It is April of 2022 and Rick is finishing up some strong chemo with multiple appointments throughout April and early May and a stem cell transplant scheduled for May/June with other infusions to follow.

A sweet nurse friend looked at me when I was telling her about all of this and she told me, "There is no testImony without a "test." As I digested that in my spirit, I told Rick that she is right.

Rick and I decided that instead of despair, we want to offer hope. We want to offer Hope"full" ness in our Hope"less"ness. We want to watch as God takes this test, yet again, and turns it into a testimony.

We truly believe that Rick will go into remission and will be healed from this cancer with many more years left here on this earth with Brian and I until the time that Jesus comes back to take us all home in the Rapture.

The discussion has come up on occasion, though, where it has been asked, "What if God heals Rick ultimately in Heaven?" What if His plan is not how you picture it? While my heart hurts to even fathom this in the earthly sense, my spirit knows that God in His infinite wisdom created us all with a time and purpose on this earth and a time to depart.

Rick and I have talked about Heaven and the joy and beauty that awaits. We have talked about seeing Jesus and our loved ones who are there waiting for us. We have talked about Brian and how he will talk to us like never before and be whole from his Autism and Seizures. Gosh, he will probably talk so much up there that no one else will ever get a chance!

While we don't anticipate that our story will end like this, we do have the hope of Heaven. We do have the assurance and the peace of eternal life in Heaven with no pain or suffering.

If God is ready for Rick to go "home" to Heaven, then Rick is ready, but he doesn't want to leave us. He told me that he knows his heart is right with God, that he would be sad to leave us here, but that he knows that he would see us again in Heaven as he would wait for us with Jesus.

So, while there is sadness in thinking of illness and tragedy and death of this life, there is also a joy in knowing that this life for all of us in only temporary. Are you prepared if something would take your life today unexpectedly? Rick and I want nothing more from our lives and our story than to reach out to you and let you know that there is a better way of living. There is a hope. There is a joy and peace that can be found even in life's most painful and difficult circumstances. God isn't finished with our story, and He isn't finished with your story yet either, my friends. If you have been given the gift of another day, then your story can be used to reach someone who is in that "pit of despair."

We want to "Stand in Faith" just as the song Danny Gokey sings that encourages us to believe in miracles that only God Himself can give. Faith. Something that you experience daily, and you may not even realize it. "Faith," ~ Every time you get in your car and turn the switch expecting it to start. "Faith," ~Every time you feel and see the effects of the wind. "Faith," ~Trusting in things that are not yet seen but knowing you will see them."

FAITH is a deep rooted yet unexplainable emotion. Sometimes, things just can't be explained. You must trust that God Supernaturally has this world and every circumstance in His hands. We must believe that He is in control and will help lead, guide, and hold us if we only choose to reach out, accept Him by faith, and allow Him to love us in the way that only He can.

As I think of a final Scripture of hope for this book, I'm reminded of Hebrews 11:1- "Faith is the substance of things HOPED for, the evidence of things not seen." Hope…. Isn't that what God has been trying to portray throughout this book?

We know that there is no "Testimony" without the "Test." There is no "Message" without the "Mess." There is no Hope"full" ness without the Hope"less"ness. I asked Rick how he wanted me to end this book. He said, "Don't." God is not finished yet." He is not done with our story. He has a plan. "Trish, God's got it." "Honey," he said, "End it with these words:"

"To
Be
Continued…"

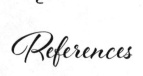

References

1). The Holy Bible, New King James Version Reference Giant Print Edition, Copyright, 2018 Harper Collins Publishing.

2). The Holy Bible, King James Version Reference Giant Print Copyright, 2017 Thomas Nelson Publishing.

3). "Hallelujah Even Here," Lydia Laird, Composers, Lydia Laird/Mia Fieldes/Jonathon Smith
Written by: Lydia Laird: Essential Music Publishing (essentialMusicPublishing.com) Copyright and Release, 2020.

4). 106.9 The Light, (thelightfm.org) Founded by Billy and Ruth Graham, 1962, Operated by Blue Ridge Broadcasting.

5). "I Will Be Here," Steven Curtis Chapman," Composer, Writer, Songwriter credit- Steven Curtis Chapman, Allan Chapman, (Universal Music Publishing Group, Capital Christian Music Group} Released, 1989 (wcisfm.org)

6). PECS, Picture Exchange Communication System- Developers: Andy Bondy, Phd and Lori Frost, MS, CCC-SLP, (Pyramid Educational Consultants, Inc., pecsusa.com), 1985.

7). ProLoQuo2Go, Adaptive Communication by AssistiveWare (assitiveware.com, 2009 initial realease date (AAC) app for iOS 2012).

8). Autism Speaks (autismspeaks.org) founded 2005.

9). Center for Disease Control (www.cdc.gov)

10). "I'll Be Home for Christmas," written by Kim Gannon and Comopsed by Walter Kent. Recording, 1943 by Bing Crosby, Released by Decca Records. (wikipedia.org)

11). "Wind Beneath My Wings", written by Jeff Silbar and Larry Henley. Originally recorded by Kamahi in 1982, then RCA Records in 1987. Latest credit sung by Bette Midler, 1989. (wikipedia.org).

12). "Amazing Grace," John Newton, 1790, Tune Name, New Britain, Harmonzier, Edwin O. Excell, 1900. Public Domain.

13). Characteristics of Eagles (linkedin.com) by Mirlande Chery, CEO Harvest Country Development, Published, September 1, 2015.

14). "Help is on the Way," Toby Mac, Composers, Micah Kulper/Toby McKeehan, Copyright, 2021- Capitol Christian Music Group, Essential Music Publishing, LLC, (essentialmusicpublishing.com).

15). "Stronger," Mandisa, Songwriters, David Garcia, Ben Glover, Christopher Stevens, Released January 2011, Sparrow Records (wikipedia.org)

16). "Stand in Faith," Danny Gokey, Composers, Mia Fieldes, Danny Gokey/Jordan Sapp, Copyright, 2021, Capitol Christian Music Group, (essentialmusicpublishing.com).

17). Healthline.org. – Definitions for Hemolacria and Hematohidrosis and researched information, "Can sweat turn into blood?"

CPSIA information can be obtained
at www.ICGtesting.com
Printed in the USA
JSHW052319030622
26637JS00002B/78